THE COLOR
CHARTREUSE, Etc.

By

Jane Hallock Combs

ISBN: 1-4033-8804-0 (e-book)
ISBN: 1-4033-8805-9 (Paperback)

Library of Congress Control Number: 2002095306

This book is printed on acid free paper.

Printed in the United States of America
Bloomington, IN

Some of these essays have appeared in "The Atlanta Constitution," "The St. Petersburg Times;" "The Rochester Democrat and Chronicle". Many have been broadcast on NPR Station WKMS, FM, Murray Ky.

1stBooks - rev. 01/02/03

To

Dave who squashed my caterpillars and saved my neck more times than I care to remember.

Acknowledgements

Thanks to long suffering, keen-eyed Margaret Vaughn for her editing, also Beverly West. Anita McNamara, Bob Cubbins and Mary Hogenson for their patient reading, help and encouragement. And special thanks to Big Sam, L'il Willie, Ceci and Lisbeth who make me laugh.

Table of Contents

Part 1 *"The Color Chartreuse"*

Part 2 *"Ya Want Some Hot Salami?"*

Part 3 "Shakespeare and Filthy Beasts"

PART 1

"THE COLOR CHARTREUSE"

Jane Hallock Combs

Mr. Dobbs' Ferry

"Dobbs Ferry. A little village in the Hudson River Valley."

That's what I tell people who ask, "Where ever did YOU come from?"

Dobbs Ferry lies about 30 miles up the Hudson River from New York City. At night, from what used to be the town dump, now Riverside Park, you can see the skyline of Manhattan and the outline of the George Washington Bridge down river. Up river, you get a view of the Tappan Zee Bridge stretching across the Hudson at Tarrytown like a graceful, sparkling necklace.

Turn the corner at the head of Dobbs Ferry's Main Street, and you look down the long slope of road that appears to end in a broad sweep of river. On a clear day you can see across to the

Jersey side with the Palisades gleaming darkly, full of vibrant colors in the morning sun.

At the head of Main street, where you turn for the Palisade view, was the old library above which a pair of famous Hollywood actors had a "love nest". That's what it was called! I always had trouble trying to imagine the squatty apartment over the musty, creaking library as being a suitable place for a Camp Fire Girl meeting, let alone a "love nest", but that's what it was called when I was a kid. Names are funny. Think of "Dobbs' Ferry." Why was it called that?

Well, obviously, a man named Dobbs had a ferry. Actually it was a small, flatbottomed boat called a periauger. I know. We named our high school year book "The Periauger" in Dobbs' honor.

Dobbs Ferry was a happening place during the American Revolution. Washington, Lafayette, Rochambeau (and anyone who wanted to cross the river from Westchester County) came there.

3

They had to take the Periauger unless they were awfully good swimmers. Mr. Dobbs and his ferry were important.

Reasons existed, though, not to name the village after Dobbs. He ran a necessary service, but stories have it he was not exactly a wildly patriotic person.

During the revolution, when everyone was taking up sides, Dobbs was taking up money from anyone who wanted to cross the river. Rebel, loyalist. You name it. Who cared as long as they had the silver? Dobbs took them across in the Periauger. It wasn't much of a boat, but it was a booming business!

After the war, when the village was incorporated, a lot of people thought the name should be changed. Surely there were some local heroes whose names would bring more honor to the village than old Dobbs who hadn't seemed to give a darn about the war, but just liked the economic opportunities it had afforded.

But for whom to name the village? There were the three fellows who had captured British spy, John Andre, when he was going through Tarrytown. He'd had a note from Benedict Arnold hidden in his boot. His captors saw him hanged for it. Why not name the village for one of the captors?

They were a brave, but mixed lot. There were problems.

Of the three *"heroes,"* one was known to be something of a lush. When he was tanked up he would beat his wife and children. Not a nice guy. Then there was the second man who was sober enough. He needed to stay sober to keep his wits about him since his major source of income seemed to be from cheating people at cards and conning unsuspecting folks out of their life's savings. That left the founding fathers with only one last candidate after whom to name the village.

5

Jane Hallock Combs

The third man was an upright sort: sober, church going, honest, kind to his family, but unfortunately with the last name of "Van Wart."

Our lovely village would have been known as "Wart-on-the Hudson." So it stayed "Dobbs Ferry." I'm glad. That's where I come from.

The Road to Heaven

The sibling relationship is an interesting one. It's the duty of older siblings to "toughen up their younger brothers and sisters so that they will be able to face life." At least that's what my brother, Dave, told me. He "toughened me up" so that I could have caught an atomic bomb in my teeth. Bless Him!

Dave specialized in playing on my fear of death. I wasn't afraid of death per se, just ETERNITY! Eternity sounded like such an exceptionally LONG time. Our nighttime prayer: "Now I lay me down to etc." didn't do a lot to comfort me. "…If I should die" before I woke… WHAMBO! I'd be in eternity!

I'd heard stuff about eternity and heaven…lots of Dave's interpretations, but it seemed to involve sitting around on clouds, plinking on harps. I didn't know how to play a harp! I played the piano, and sitting around on a cloud FOREVER didn't sound so great. What could we really DO there? It bothered me a lot when I was three years old. I used to lie awake nights worrying about it.

Recently I came across an old diary of my mother's written the year I was three. It was full of notations such as, "Jane was awake again last night worried about dying. Ayyh!"

My mother's diary entries concerning me frequently ended in the expression, "Ayyh!" I believe it was a term of endearment.

Anyway, I would press Dave during the sunny daytime to expand on heaven. I wanted to know EXACTLY where it was, and precisely how you got there. Dave showed me.

At the bottom of our hill, where we always turned to go to Mama Losago's grocery, was a huge tar patch where tar had drooled down the road and collected in a broad puddle. On hot days, the tar would develop interesting little bubbles you could pop with your white sneakers. A wonderful activity on hot summer afternoons. Didn't do much for white sneakers though.

On one afternoon, as I sat down to rest for a bit on the grass next to the hot tar patch, I noticed a twisting road that went off at a tangent from the one that led to Losago's grocery. The tangent road wound up a gradual hill weaving back and forth before eventually disappearing over the crest of the hill.

"What's that road?" I asked Dave who was still pouncing on tar bubbles. "Where does it go?"

Dave saw an opportunity. He jumped onto it.

"That's the road to heaven!"

My eyes bugged out. "Really?"

"Would I lie to my little sister?"

"But look!" I pointed. "There's a car going up there!"

"Sure," Dave instructed. "They're dead. They're on their way to heaven."

Hm-m-m!" Big brothers sure knew everything!

My absorption with death didn't last much longer. My mother was getting tired of sleepless nights spent comforting a three year old who didn't want to die. Mama, who was very practical, settled the matter by telling me I didn't have to die if I didn't want to. When I became old, I could just go to the "Old Folks Home." Now that had possibilities! They'd probably have a piano there and comfortable couches. No trying to balance on a cloud with a dumb harp!

I saw the entry in my mother's diary where she wrote, "Finally got Jane settled by telling her she could go to the old folks home as an alternative to dying. Maybe we'll get some sleep tonight! Ayyh!"

It worked in spite of the fact that I was reminded of death every time I would see a car making its way up the hilly road to heaven. Sometimes I'd wave good-bye to the poor souls who obviously didn't know about the "Old Folk's" home.

It did come as a shock to me though, the day I started kindergarten. The bus pulled up to the tar patch, and I climbed on in my new, starched jumper dress. I sat down, glanced out the window and then gasped as the bus, instead of turning left toward Losego's grocery and downtown, slowly started up the curvy road to heaven! Ayhh!

The road led not to *heaven*, but to the Dobbs Ferry School.

Yes, the sibling relationship is an interesting one. But I had the last laugh. I never told Dave about the Old Folk's Home!

Jane Hallock Combs

The Real Santa Claus

When I was five, I knew what Santa Claus was supposed to look like. Moreover, I knew what he was supposed to *be* like. Santa knew all about little kids. We didn't have to explain *anything to him!*

The day I caused the rumpus in Macy's, I'd been warned by my brother about fake Santas. Dave had a cold and couldn't go with us into the city on our Christmas shopping spree.

"Don't be fooled if he looks like Santa." Dave had said. "It might be just some regular guy with pillows stuffed up his shirt and a fake beard on his chin!"

Dave elaborated: "You can always tell a fake beard ... It's got little hooks that go over the ears."

Santa Claus was on Macy's fifth floor. I loved going up the escalators, but I hated the way my mother kept such a tight grip on my wrist.

When I complained about it, she whispered fiercely to me, "If I let loose of you for one minute, you disappear! You know it, and *I know it!*"

Just because I'd slipped away from her a few times in the past and gone exploring on my own, she didn't trust me. I was *never lost.* I always knew where I was!

Mama gave me a dollar bill for the entry fee to *The Magic Tunnel of Christmas* where a "people mover" (referred to as "the Magic Carpet") would whisk me away to Santa Claus.

"This nice Elf will show you the way," Mother said.

A scruffy looking little man in a worn red and green elf suit cranked up a smile that made him look like he'd just eaten a fuzzy worm.

"Ho-HO-Ho! Little Goil," he said in a decidedly Bronx accent, as he snatched my dollar entry fee, giving me a ticket and a little shove onto the Magic Carpet. "This here bea-yu-ti-ful magic carpet will take youse tru da secret tunnel right to Santa' Magic Woik Shop!"

There was a line of kids ahead of me already on the *Magic Carpet*...a couple of them crying for their mothers. Other kids were jockeying for position trying to get the first glimpse of Santa.

Suddenly, the *Magic Carpet* burst out of the *Secret Tunnel* and THERE HE WAS sitting in a regal red chair, surrounded by elves of various sizes wearing outfits with hats that had long hanging pompoms swinging from the tops.

Santa looked real all right. As the line grew closer, I could see that his beard looked real too. The little hooks going over his ears could be from his glasses.

"Move it up there, Kids," another pushy elf with a touch of the Bronx about him was trying to speed up the line.

"And lets keep that loine straight, ho-ho-ho!"

His Ho's sounded a little cross

The kids didn't have much time with Santa. It seemed like they popped up on his lap, said two words, heard some "Ho-ho's," then they were shuffled off with a striped candy cane to "Exit through dat der door."

Then it was MY turn. My mother had paid a whole dollar for me to go in there. I wanted to get my money's worth.

Old Cranky Elf helped me up on Santa's lap. Santa sure LOOKED fat.

I hit my sharp elbow into his stomach. It didn't feel like pillows!

"Ouch, Kid!" said Santa. "Watch it, OK?"

He threw in a Ho or so then went on in a bored voice,"So Whatdayawant for Christmas?"

There was something about him that was making me suspicious … but I told him my heart's desire:

"I want a Betsy Wetsy!"

"A what?"

"A BETSY WETSY!"

"I'll try to get it. Ho Ho Ho … Whatever it is!

"You don't know what a Betsy Wetsy is?"

This time I poked his stomach, hard, and then grabbed his beard which pulled down from his ears then snapped back with a "sproing-g!" when I let it go. FAKE!

"You're not Santa!" I shouted, sliding off his lap. "You're just a big, fat man with FAKE whiskers. Taking money from little kids!"

I stuck my face up to his, "I want my dollar back!"

The elf was shoving candy canes at me and trying to calm down the rest of kids who were starting to come unglued en masse and looked as though they might stampede at any moment.

"He's not Santa!" I shouted to the other kids, "Get your money back! It's a gyp!"

By the time the Elves had gotten me (and about a dozen other sobbing kids) out of there, my waiting mother grabbed me demanding, "Janie what did you DO in there?

"He was NOT Santa, Mama, "I said handing her back the crumpled dollar I'd finally been given to shut me up.

"He never even HEARD of Betsy Wetsy!"

"...And I don't want to hear about her ever again," Momma said.

"The Real Santa will get me one!" I pouted as my mother pulled me away.

"Over my dead body!" Mama was cross.

I don't remember much else about that Christmas, but I do know that the real Santa Claus brought me a Betsy Wetsy. I remember my mother rolled her eyes (she did that a lot!) But my Dad winked at me. I think he believed in Santa too!

17

Gang of Eight

It embarrassed my mother when the police came looking for my brother, Dave, and me. It was because of the stage coach. The gang had found it over by the fields near the Litster Estate.

The fields were our territory. That's where the boys played touch football and there Dave broke his leg the summer someone touched a tad hard.

The field was also where Nancy Cowles and I always picked huge bouquets of black-eyed Susans for our mothers and where we had held the big "fair" with tents rigged up on poles and everything from fortune tellers to games of chance and daring do … Toss a loop at a penny a toss … win one of the Cowles' kittens. The kittens were also billed as "the man eating lions." They were almost out of the kitten stage by then and being manhandled by the gang had made picking up one of the sharp clawed kittens a definite feat of daring do.

Yes, the field was the gang's turf ... the place where we most usually could be found by searching parents ... or, I guess, the police.

I don't know who discovered the stage coach, but the word went out about it that warm August day to the whole Gang (including Nancy and me who were distinctly low on the totem pole). Anyway the Gang congregated on the rocks beyond Grandpa O'Dell's to discuss the stage coach.

The "big kids" had found a genuine stage coach, obviously abandoned, next to the white gravel road that led up the hill to the Litster Estate. It sat on the curve of the road at the edge of the green grass right before you got to the gates leading into the estate.

The coach had an old bushel basket full of flowers sitting on the driver's seat. Almost like a decoration, but who would waste a perfectly

19

good, genuine stage coach using it as a decoration?

Sam Brown, Zip Zipfield and the other "big kids" had managed to jiggle the coach loose from the rocks that were on either side of its wheels. They had dragged it across the white gravel road onto the "field" proper by the time we got there. We opened the doors and climbed in. Nancy and I thought it was more like a fancy carriage from old movies with ladies and dukes and all. There was even a metal vase hanging inside one of the doors. You could put a flower in it. It was a CARRIAGE!

The boys said we were nuts. Anyone could see it was definitely a stage coach, and when they finished restoring it we'd see it too.

Grandpa O'Dell would probably let us use his barn for the fix-up, if we could get the coach there. It took all eight of us to bounce it through the field to the path that led to the stone wall. The path was tricky because there were bushes and young trees close to the path. The path ran right through the middle of prickers and branches. The doors would get scratched the way WE always did.

'No problem," Zip, our leader, said, "We"ll take the doors off! We can put them back on later."

The bigger boys had to work at it a bit but they finally got the doors torn off. They splintered awfully easily. Nancy and I felt bad. The doors were ruined. So was the neat little flower vase! We'd had plans for that.

Trying to maneuver the coach along the narrow, winding path was rough. It fell over a couple of times and we had a lot of trouble getting it upright again. Little pieces of stuff kept falling off the coach. The path was a mess!

When we got to the wall, we were all sweaty and tired. The wall looked like more of an obstacle than we had expected.

"Geez," Zip exploded, "how are we ever going to get it over the wall?"

"Easy", Sam the second in command, offered. "We got the doors off, didn't we?" Nancy and I glanced back to where the doors, a splintered disaster, were now lying haphazard and abandoned beside the path. "We'll just take the rest of it apart. We can carry it to Grandpa's barn in pieces, then put it back together!" The big boys were always optimistic.

My memory has a small glitch here. I'm not sure what happened next. I know the stage coach WAS taken apart. Probably Nancy and I had been left out because we had no tools, and we were too little to be much help anyway. I think we went home and had a tea party. I don't know what my brother did.

I do remember when the police came to the house and asked to speak with us. They were surprised to find that two of the culprits, part of a "gang that had taken a valuable, antique coach belonging to the Litster Estate" were aged three and four and were currently deeply involved in a tea party with their dolls. We got off. So did Dave, who was six. The police thought the whole thing pretty funny. My mother was embarrassed. The police finally figured professionals had taken the carriage away in a truck. Little kids couldn't have been involved in something of that magnitude.

A few years ago, Dave told me that when they heard the police were looking for the missing carriage, the big kids had become frightened. They'd dug a huge hole at the edge of the path through the woods and buried the pieces, packing sod and pine needles over it. It was never found.

Battle of the Apple Orchard

When the Italians attacked, Nancy and I were hiding behind a wall. We'd been there forever it seemed, though it was probably only minutes. The tension before a battle is so horrific time does cartwheels!

We weren't often in the battles. This was the first one. The others had been more like skirmishes. There hadn't been a need to involve us in them, but when word came that Rocky Moritelli's gang was on the move up from Dobbs Ferry, Nancy and I were called in. That showed how desperate the situation was. We were not usually alerted.

The leader of the "Hill Gang" looked down on us as the "little girls." To my brother I would ALWAYS be "a little girl." Not until I achieved whatever age he was then would I be considered "big." However, when I got *there*, he was again three years older than I, and I would be given a new goal to shoot for. But the night the Italians attacked, I was given a chance to prove my mettle.

"Just stay behind that wall and holler when they come creeping around. We'll do the hard stuff."

Rocky and his gang were coming up to steal apples from Grandpa O'dell's orchard. They had no right! Grandpa O'dell's orchard was our turf! For years Grandpa O'Dell had looked the other way when my brother and his gang helped themselves to the luscious fruit hanging ripe from Grandpa's trees. Actually he encouraged us and would point out which apples were the sweetest and which cherries had ripened to the peak of perfection and, important to Nancy and me, where we "little kids" could find the best apples already on the ground. He'd occasionally boost a smaller child up to a cherry branch that was a teensy bit out of reach, and then wait to assure himself we got back down again safely.

Grandpa Odell was an old gentleman who was kind to children probably because his own two children, then middle aged people, were both retarded. Viola and Charlie often played with us kids, but on the night of the "Battle of the Orchard," they were nowhere around. Neither was Grandpa O'Dell.

The sun was going down, and shadows were lengthening. We shivered. Nancy and I began to think about hot cocoa and bed. Then I saw it.

There was a shadow beside the Northern Spy apple tree. A shadow that was moving slowly, but steadily. Another shadow crept along behind it. A last sliver of sunlight illuminated curly hair and an unfamiliar face.

The Italians were here! There was no sign of David and "our gang." Then lying on the ground near me I spotted a broken limb from one of the constantly tormented trees. I grabbed it, and with a scream like a skinned cat, jumped out from behind the wall, wielding my clumsy weapon, swinging about at any and all intruders with the power and fury of your average, enraged, six year old.

"Yowl!" I had made contact with someone's rear.

David and our guys jumped down out of the Winesap and Mackintosh trees and began pelting Rocky Moretelli's gang with windfalls we had gathered in piles like snow balls.

The battle was over shortly. Really just another skirmish.

"But did you see my sister!" David's voice dripped with pride. "Did you see her with that stick? She's a terror!" David rubbed my head in the ultimate token of brotherly esteem. "That was *Rocky* you got," he said, punching me good naturedly in the arm ... I'd have a bruise for a month. "You gave him a good one, right across his ole butt!"

David promised me that night that as soon as I was a really "big girl" I could become a full fledged member of the gang. I rubbed my arm deciding maybe I should rethink the whole thing.

"How old do *I HAVE TO BE?*" I asked.

"Nine!" he answered. And I believed him.

When I was nine the gang was a thing of the past, and both David and Rocky were into football and Boy Scouts.

I'm going back to Dobbs Ferry next month for our high school reunion. The first night of the reunion we're all going out for Pizza at "Scappies" (the only place in the universe for real pizza). I wonder if Rocky will be there. I wonder if he remembers The Battle of The Apple Orchard.

Probably not.

I hope not.

The Color Chartreuse

Yesterday, I found a black and yellow striped caterpillar on the back deck. I'd collected these caterpillars when I was a kid. I don't know their technical name, but, for some reason, I had always called them all "Jeffries."

Feeling like a child again, I picked this little fellow up, laughed and called him "Jeffrey" as he tickled and inched his way across my hand like so many of his predecessors years ago. I watched his little feet go up and down in perfect synchronization ... and I suddenly remembered why I have never liked the color chartreuse.

I'd always liked caterpillars. When I was six, I'd had a rather extensive collection of Jeffries in an old cigar box under my bed. My mother did not think much of my collection. Sure, Mama was a nature lover ... in its place ... in the garden, but she didn't really appreciate my Jeffries.

Jane Hallock Combs

I know that a caterpillar getting into the popcorn at the movies, and Mama being the lucky recipient of it had been unfortunate, but that had been an accident, and my "Jeffries" weren't as difficult to deal with as the praying mantis' babies had been.

I'd found this wonderful translucent cocoon in the fields and just knew it contained a caterpillar en route to a glorious existence as a butterfly. I planned to watch the butterfly hatch. I put it in a sunny spot on the dining room window next to my mother's prize African violets. Mama didn't know about the cocoon until the hatching.

Daily I checked it and was crushed when, instead of a gorgeous butterfly emerging, eight hundred and sixty eight praying mantis babies (more or less) popped out and immediately assumed prayerful positions all over our dining room...mostly on the windows and the African violets.

I remember how really interesting the window looked with the little creatures all over it. Sort of like a lacy, living curtain. Mama was not thrilled!

It took us forever to get the prayful ones out of the house. Surprising how fast praying mantises grow. Surprising how irritated my normally calm mother could become. Especially when I accidentally knocked over her "Pink Cotton Candy" violet that had just begun to bloom after years of false starts.

Lots of prayers, mine and the bugs', were said over it. It didn't help.

No! My Jeffries were definitely a lot less trouble than the mantises, popcorn incident aside. I could easily carry my caterpillar loaded cigar box around, or just take the individual Jeffrey with me on my regular jaunts across our fields and woods … letting them tippytoe across my hand as I walked.

I liked the Jeffries' sense of determination and concentration as they would hunch their way across my hand lifting their multitudinous little feet one at a time in an organized way that boggled my imagination.

How would it feel to have so many feet to keep track of? What if the next to last foot on the left side got out of step? Would the caterpillar stumble and fall on its small face? I was intrigued.

I had been walking one day, having a chat with a Jeffrey, when I ran into my big brother, who, like Mama, was not enchanted with my caterpillars.

"Now what are you doing with that dumb thing?"

I tried to educate David. I held my hand up and said:

"Look at this Jeffrey. Look at the way he walks. It's like a little wave going across my hand."

"And why do you have to call them all "Jeffries"? They're just stupid caterpillars!"

"I LIKE to call them Jeffries!" I held my hand up so David could see better. "Look at him! He's so cute!"

With that, nine year old David lifted his big, callused, boy's hand and slammed it down onto mine.

Suddenly my hand was a mess of chartreuse.

"Now he's cute!" David laughed as I looked at the oozing remains of my Jeffrey.

It took me a long time to forgive my brother for that. I look at the yellow and black caterpillar crawling across my hand now, and remember a forgotten pain … and a hatred of the color chartreuse.

Jane Hallock Combs

Leprosy

There hadn't been an outbreak of leprosy in Dobbs Ferry for a long time, but I didn't know that. The shiny spot on the tip of my finger was something new. I sat in Miss Spellman's first grade class during spelling and looked at it. The whirl of my fingerprint was gone. There was only this shiny, slick place that had no feeling to it when I would poke it with the point of my pencil. Leprosy for sure!

We'd been learning about leprosy in Sunday School. I knew the scenario. First a little place of deadness like this terrifying, shiny spot, and then my finger tip would fall off. Then an ear maybe, or my left eyebrow would end up in my soup.

I poked the dead spot again with my pencil. No feeling! That was it! I had leprosy! I was dying!

A bell rang. Time for recess. Everybody jumped out of their seats and headed toward the door. Petey Thomkin gave me a friendly bat on the back of the head as he went by and said, "Hey, Hallock! Gotcha last!" The room emptied like a balloon that had been pricked.

"Jane," Miss Spellman called from the door, "Come on, time for recess. What's the matter?"

She noticed that I had put my head down on my desk and was starting to bawl. Miss Spellman came over to me. "Well, what is it?" She asked.

I looked up at her kind face and blubbered, "I've got leprosy. I'm dying!" I held up my index finger with its tell-tale shiny spot and let her have the full impact of my tragedy.

She laughed. I hadn't ever known her to so be heartless before. How could you laugh at a poor little first grader with leprosy?

"Looks like you've burned yourself on something." she said, holding my finger in her warm hand. I remember her beautiful nails … painted pale pink. I loved her.

"Do you remember touching the stove or anything hot?" She asked.

It came back to me. Mama had let me help with the ironing over the weekend. She'd shown me how to iron the napkins, smoothing them just so with the hot iron, then folding them in half, smoothing them again, and repeating the process. I remembered licking my finger and tapping it on the hot iron bottom the way Mama had shown me to check on the iron's temperature. A couple of times I hadn't gotten my finger wet enough, or I had left it on the iron more than the millisecond necessary for checking it. It had hurt. But not much and I'd forgotten about it.

I told Miss Spellman, and then asked, "Do you think that's what it could be?"

"Probably," she answered, "but I'm *absolutely certain* your spot isn't leprosy."

She patted my hand, wiping my face with her lace trimmed hankie that smelled hauntingly of lavender, then sent me out to the playground.

I thought about that incident recently as I spent time locked up in the Medville County Hospital trying to find out what had caused me to leave a good movie to go to the emergency room. I had felt as though an elephant had stepped on my chest.

Whoops! I thought. Heart attack. Pressure and pain in the middle of my being. Typical. What else could it be?

The pain was bad, but only lasted about forty minutes. By the time I'd gotten to the emergency room, had an aspirin to chew on, a nitro tablet under the tongue and an IV dripping heparin into my system, I was feeling pretty perky.

Three days later, I felt a lot less perky after having what seemed like quarts of blood siphoned out of my body (mostly during the night immediately after I'd fall asleep, when I did sleep, on a mattress that was a little more comfortable than sleeping on rocks.) But lots of tests had shown that my heart hadn't been the culprit. Rather it seems some nasty little germs who spend their time causing ulcers and stomach reflux, etc. had taken up residence in my innards. They occasionally try to impress people with their strength by mocking a heart attack. They do a good job.

Fortunately there is a medication which will kill these little buggers, and I returned home with a little bottle of pills which should do the trick. I feel great now.

It's nice not to have had a heart attack. It was nice also not to have had leprosy.

When the Going Gets Tough!

They say, "When the going gets tough, the tough get going!"

I must be pretty tough. I can tell because whenever things get the teentsiest bit out of hand, my basic, gut reaction always is, "Well, I'm OUT OF HERE!"

I've always been fleet on my feet. Early memories of my parents' voices echo the refrain, "Where IS Jane, anyway. She was here a minute ago". This usually said when there were dishes to be done, table to be set, bed to be made. They referred to it as my "disappearing act."

Now, dishes and bed making were a pain, but then there were the truly more difficult situations which I seemed to manage to evade with my quick side step skills. Like the day my mother dropped me at the dentist's office.

Old Doc Marshall had me ensconced in his big chair, bib clipped around my seven year old neck, cotton rolls wedged around my teeth. Then he made the classic mistake. He took his eyes off me for a moment and turned to rearrange some instruments on his tray. By the time he turned back, the chair was empty and only a breeze filled the room. I was halfway up Ashford Avenue, sneakered feet flying, paper bib flapping, spitting a trail of cotton balls … on my way home! Doc Marshall wasn't happy. Neither were my parents. But they all agreed I could move fast.

Good thing. Lots of folks had occasion to want to catch me for one reason or another. Like during my "pink period."

I had nagged forever (or maybe six months which is the same as forever for a child) to be allowed to take ballet lessons. I KNEW I was a dancer. I felt it in my bones. My mother frequently found me dancing around the kitchen when I was supposed to be ironing the napkins or drying the dishes. My Philco radio blared while I jumped around, skinny legs pointing, bony arms flailing the air. Grace personified!

Mama gave in eventually and let me take ballet lessons. But INSULT OF INSULTS ... the teacher didn't recognize a budding ballerina when she saw one. The first week she started me off with *flat black slippers* and a bunch of *exercises*.! I didn't want exercises and FLAT BLACK SLIPPERS! I wanted tour jetés, a frothy TUTU and pink toe shoes with matching ribbons that would wrap around my stick legs, turning me into a pink Degas ballerina like the print I had scotch taped to the back of my bedroom door.

The first two lessons I spent arguing with the teacher. Mrs. Tishman would explain to me carefully that I could not go directly up "on point," as she called it, due to my immature muscles and weak feet.

Weak, heck! I could pick up a Tootsie Roll or a hardened wad of gum with my bare toes! I was working on grabbing golf balls and could do it if my toes were little longer ... but Mrs. Tishman was unpersuasible. No toe shoes yet!

There were all these positions we had to arrange ourselves into ... then do squats called "Pliés!"

Did she call this dancing? Where had she learned about dancing? Dancing was whirling, twirling, pointing your toes (in glamorous pink toe shoes laced half way up your legs). Dancing was leaping across the room in tune with music ... REAL MUSIC ... not squatting up and down to the count of three while some do-do beat out time on a tinny piano.

My third lesson was crisis time. I gave Mrs. Tishman one more opportunity to let me have toe shoes. I took off my sock and wiggled my foot in her face then, dropping a yellow, number two pencil on the floor, tried to awe her with my ability to pick it up with my toes. She was underwhelmed.

"We're not going to talk about it ANYMORE, Jane," She said. "So, put on your nice, little, black slippers NOW! You'll go on point when you are ready and NOT BEFORE!"

Well, I showed her! The minute her back was turned, I was out that door and half way down the street bare feet flying.

My mother was surprised to see me come leaping in the back door, but she wasn't very sympathetic … and she never let me take dancing lessons again.

So … I never became a dancer, but I still retain my same, basic determination … I know. Things have been difficult around here lately. But you know what the tough do when the going gets tough. If you see a flash of light, don't worry. It's just me … heading out for Minnesota!

Forgetfulness

I'm down now to only one glove. Considering that I bought four pair last Fall, the discovery of the singular glove tells me it must be almost Spring. Amazing they lasted as long as they did. I lose things. My friends think my mind, but that's not true. That's about the only thing I haven't lost ... yet.

I frequently misplace my keys. Well, who doesn't? I ALWAYS go through at least three pair of gloves a year.

I lost my hat during the Humane Society fund raiser this year and the time spent with people looking for it probably cost the humane folks a thousand dollars or so.

I misplace cups of coffee, my glasses, occasionally my car and frequently my purse or wallet.

Walmart knows my phone number by heart because they are always calling me to tell me someone has retrieved my purse from a shopping cart somewhere. Inept (or beginning) thieves follow me around with a look of joyous anticipation on their faces. They figure it's only a matter of time before I leave a money packed purse in their vicinity. My purses are NEVER packed with money. I know myself too well. I may be forgetful, but I am not stupid.

At least when I had babies, I never misplaced them! I know several people who did. Ursa Lou Jones left her youngest in a shopping cart and didn't discover her mistake until she got home. And my friend, Thatcher, was always misplacing little Luly. Thatcher was a brilliant lawyer and a marvelous conversationalist, but several times when we would be visiting I would realize that I hadn't seen baby Luly in a while.

"Thatcher," I'd say stopping her in the middle of a tale of court intrigue, "where is little Luly, anyway? I haven't seen her for a bit."

"Oh yes," Thatcher would say, "I think I was changing her dydie upstairs. Yes that's it. That's where she must be"

We'd rush upstairs to find little Luly crawling around perilously close to:

      a. the edge of the bed,

      b. the top of the stairs,

      c. the cord to the hot iron, or

      d. the tail of the ill tempered cat.

Visiting Thatcher was always exciting.

I never lose people, only things.

That's OK. I was impressed with the Hansel and Gretal story. Like them, I leave a trail of stuff behind me. It may some time lead me home, or somewhere!

"*I AM NOT GOING SENILE!*" I tell my friends. "I've always been like this!'

And it's true. I don't remember losing my teething ring, but I do remember the time when I was seven; I went to Blue Lake with my friend Nancy Cowles and her family. We swam and played in the sun and had a picnic on the beach. Then, when it was time to leave, Nancy and I dashed to the little communal ladies dressing room, changed out of our wet suits and ran to the Cowles' car. As we settled ourselves in the backseat for the return ride home, I noticed the vinyl seat was a tad cool.

"Oops," I hollered. "Stop the car!" Mr. Cowles had just started backing out of the parking lot. "I forgot my panties!" I hopped out, ran to the dressing room, slipped into my pink Monday ones (though I think the day was a Thursday), then ran back to the car.

It was a silly childhood mistake, but one Mr. Cowles NEVER let me forget. The Cowleses were close friends of our family, and we took many little automobile trips to many places during the years, but I don't believe there ever was a time that I got into the Cowles car without Mr. Cowles asking me,

"Now, Janie, are you sure you have your panties?"

It was embarrassing when I was a teenager, but now I don't worry about my forgetfulness. As my friends say,

"Well, that's just Jane all over!"

A Close Encounter with General de Gaulle

(Note: This was written during the time when our then President Clinton was having his problems with the Monica business. Talk of the President and sex seemed to pop up everywhere…even at the family table!)

The morning of my encounter with General de Gaulle, sex had not been a hot topic at our family breakfast table. It never was. I assume my parents had sex at least a *couple* of times. It was just not a conversational topic at meals.

We didn't talk about sex, but we did talk about our President … AND General de Gaulle's scheduled visit to FDR at his home in Hyde Park that same day.

"He's going to go right up the parkway. We'll be able to see him easy!"

My brother, Dave, was so excited he hadn't noticed I'd grabbed the last sausage from the platter.

49

"He'll go right between Dobbs Ferry and Ardsley. There'll be a motorcade, and everything! Everybody's going to be there."

I savored the sausage, then added:.

"Can we go, Mom? Can we, huh?"

I thought about the tall French General who wore the funny, pillbox hat. He was always in the newsreels and newspapers. Now he'd be coming up our Sawmill River Parkway!

Motorcades carrying dignitaries often went up the parkway en route to Hyde Park. At times FDR himself would go roaring along in his long, black limousine announced by sirens and flanked by motorcycle police in their shiny helmets and sharp uniforms. It was always exciting.

Late at night I would sometimes hear the sirens going up the parkway and know that the President, Churchill, or *someone* was heading for Hyde Park.

"We'd better get going early if we want to see anything," Mom said as she began clearing the table.

The intersection of the Parkway and Lefurgy Ave. wasn't far from our house, so we hustled down Lefurgy before the crowds got too big. The police had already blocked off entrances to the Parkway. We knew we didn't have long to wait.

"Boy! We've got a great spot!" Dave grinned, checking out our line of sight, but as more and more people arrived to watch for de Gaulle, there was jostling for position. Before I knew it, I was separated from Dave and Mom. I could see nothing but a sea of legs. Who wanted to see legs? I wanted to see de Gaulle!

I tried wiggling my way back in closer to the Parkway but it was impossible. I edged down as far as I could to the right of the intersection, but couldn't even see the road! We'd hear the sirens soon. I was going to MISS the whole thing! Then I had an inspiration.

A path runs through the hills and trees parallel to the parkway … part of the Appalachian Trail. My friends and I had ridden our bikes along the path a couple of times taking a short cut down to my Grandma Hallock's in Nepera Park. I wasn't supposed to go that way alone, but this was an EMERGENCY! I shot out for the path, racing along it as fast as any rabbit.

In a few minutes, I came to a stretch of the parkway with only trees and flowering bushes. *No people!* Still further, and I'd found a place where I had a perfectly clear view of the parkway stretching at least a half mile with no one in sight.

I'd just finished wiping the sweat from my face and retying the bow on one of my pigtails when I heard the distant sounds of the motorcade. They'd passed Nepera Park and were headed my way!

Running my hand under my nose, then brushing the dust off my shorts, I pulled myself up straight and assumed my position of honor beside the Parkway.

"Alons enfants de la patria ..." I began singing in my quaverly little voice the song my mother had taught me, "The Marseillaise"... the French National Anthem!

As the first motorcycle police came into view, I sang louder snapping myself to even straighter attention, lifting my right hand in a smart "Camp Fire Girl" salute. Three fingers held stiffly to my forehead, I continued belting out "The Marseillaise": *La jour de gloire est arrive!"* Pretty it may not have been, but LOUD it was!

The motorcycles led a black convertible which slowed noticeably as it approached my vantage point.

As the car came closer, I sang my loudest and proudest while my knobby knees shook with excitement. The car slowed to a crawl, then I saw the large man in the back seat stare at me. He unwound his long body pulling himself up to a stand. The little pill box hat sat squarely in the middle of his head above the long, Gallic nose.

In one of the happiest, proudest moments of my life, the car passed me as General Charles de Gaulle, the head of Free France, raised his big hand to his forehead and saluted ME ... a seven year Camp Fire Girl singing the "Marseillaise"!

In Praise of Pickles

Pickles are wonderful creations! I've always loved them, any size, shape, or denomination! I believe when I was weaned, I went directly onto pickles. Pickled herring, pickled onions, pickled dills. It's all the same to me. Something about that wild, pickle flavor makes my taste buds burst into full bloom.

Only once did pickles really get me into trouble.

I was eight when my family went to the New York World's Fair. I still have a picture of the four of us, hand in hand, me wearing my best flower-trimmed organdy dress, (the same dress I had worn when I'd bombed out at Mrs. Teaman's piano recital). The dress brings back traumatic memories.

Also in the picture is a distinguished looking gentleman, the owner, I believe, of a large, redwood company on the West-Coast. He had done business with my father for years and was visiting the city. He wanted to take us to the World's Fair. He planned to treat us to dinner at one of the fair's finest restaurants. What fun!

I remember being warned to be on my best behavior. I should mind my manners and, "For Heavens sakes … *don't speak unless spoken to!*"

Mama always had to remind me of the only time that same gentleman had come to our house for dinner.

Mama had created a feast with Steak and Kidney Pie … a luxury at the time.

"There'a a long hair in my food!" I had blurted out, lifting up the offending strand still dripping gravy.

"Now, Jane," said my embarrassed red-haired mother, "it must be one of yours."

"No, it's not!" I said, waving the offending hair around in case anyone had missed it the first time. "It's red! It's yours!" *My hair* was blond.

Mr. Plant, bless him, ignored the contretemps between me and my mother. He went so far as to ask for a second helping of meat pie.

But now, at the World's Fair I was on warning!

"Be good! Be polite, and WATCH WHAT YOU SAY!"

We were going to eat at a Swedish restaurant, a very *costly Swedish restaurant,*. It was the first smorgasbord I'd ever heard of, let alone seen!

Unfortunately, after we got into the crowded, *pricey* smorgasbord, I became separated from my parents. I often did. No problem. I had my plate, and I had been apprised of the procedure.

Weaving my way between the crowds of grown-ups, I saw the table. Stretching the length of the room, it brimmed over with food of every sort: delectable, browned meats with little frilly paper decorations on each bone; vegetables in succulent sauces; sizzling potatoes; and salads of every variety;...*and PICKLES!*

I hadn't known the Scandanavians were such pickle people. It was obvious.

There were pickled beets, pickled eggs, pickled fish of every discription, and one million, two hundred and ninety different pickled vegetables and fruits.

Before my mother could discern where I was and catch my eye with her extremely baleful one, I had managed to load my entire plate with every type of pickle known to man.

It was a balanced meal really. I had pickled fish, pickled vegetables … lots of them, and even pickled fruit. How balanced can you get?

I heard about that episode for years afterwards, but it didn't deter me from my love of pickles.

I, of course, tried making my own. OK, but not as good as my all time favorite Heinz Dills (pickled in wood). I used to buy large jars of them. When they were gone, I saved the juice. Later I would slice up fresh cucumbers or other veggies into it. In a couple of days, they were delicious!

I always had an extra jar of pickle juice sitting in the fridge waiting for incipient pickles. I never thought it could cause a problem. My kids were always under the strict edict NEVER to throw away the pickle juice when the last pickle was eaten. I suspect I never explained why.

It was several years after my daughter Amy married that she came to me asking:

"Mom, why do you always save old pickle juice?"

I explained. She heaved a huge sigh of relief. It seemed she and her sister, Robin, had been religiously saving old pickle juice in their *own* refrigerators after marriage, but had never known why. They only knew their Mama had said it was a law! Pickle juice should NEVER BE THROWN OUT! They only discarded it when it was gray and moldy.

They're good kids, but not as sharp as pickles.

Jane Hallock Combs

Silver Rings and Indian Dresses

My friend, Norma, owns an antique shop. On my umpteenth birthday she gave me a small package wrapped in tissue.

"You'll never guess what it is!" She said. It was an odd shape. It felt like a ring. I felt it carefully then and knew what it was! I hadn't seen one in a million years ... but I *knew!*

"It's a Camp Fire Girl's ring!" I blurted out as I tore the tissue off to reveal a small silver ring with the tell-tale bundle of silver twigs held together by silver "sinews." Three raised dots on either side of the "bundle" stood for the credo of the Camp-Fire-Girls, "Work, Health, Love" ("Wo-He-Lo"... the secret Camp-Fire-Girl pass word!)

Norma, who knew I'd been a Camp Fire Girl, had seized on the ring when it came into her shop and now it was mine. I slipped it on my pinky finger … no longer a person of an obscene age, but a kid eight years old again!

Are the Camp Fire Girls still in existence? I don't know, but the troop in Dobbs Ferry was founded by Mrs. Pennysworth, mother of my best friend, Patsy. We had rounded up six or seven girls from the fourth grade all of whom felt as we did … that Girl Scouting looked dull and the Girl Scout uniforms duller.

The Camp Fire Girl uniforms influenced us a lot. They were cute. Navy blue skirts, white shirts and classy little red neckerchiefs. *That* was just our *every day meeting uniforms*. We were all going to have *Indian Outfits* too! Long, fringed, leathery affairs complete with beaded headbands. I believe we were to add feathers as we achieved our Indian goals. None of us ever did get our Indian outfits, but we WERE Indians. That was the exciting part. We got to learn Indian lore, study Indian symbols and, best of all, have AUTHENTIC Indian names and personal *symbols*!

My name was Tawanca ("Laughing Water"). My symbol was a huge V with a lightning bolt running through it. The whole thing perched on top of a straight line with a wavy one under it. All hush-hush! We could sign our symbols to notes, and no one but another Camp-Fire-Girl would know who wrote the note. That is, if they could remember which symbol meant which girl! We were sort of a confused lot. But we all had our little silver rings, our Indian names, and our secret signs!

Mrs. Pennysworth tried to involve us in worthwhile projects. We were deeply involved in trying to bead our headbands. Not an easy task. On our little looms we would have to line up tiny beads with our eight year old fingers, then try to get a needle through the beads on top of the loom threads. It took about an hour and a half to get one row of beads in right. And beads were always spilling!

I worked on my head band for about a month before I had completed a half an inch. The center of the headband with the designs and my personal symbol on it was as least a year or more away.

Also the authentic leatherette Indian costumes with fringe and fancy stuff seemed an impossible dream. They were expensive and none of our Indian group had parents ready or willing to spring for a second, more expensive "ceremonial" uniform.

Our meetings degenerated into giggle sessions, marshmallow roasts and bead hunts. Some one always managed to spill their beads all over the floor. We'd have to hunt them frequently scrunching glass beads into Mrs. Pennysworth carpets and floors.

I'm not sure how we disbanded. I think Mrs. Pennysworth finally had enough of little girls whose main interest in Camp Firing involved cooking marshmallows until they were black and fussing about not having real Indian dresses. Not one of us had been able to get a leatherette "ceremonial" dress. Big disappointment!

Time passed, and then a couple of years ago, at a golf resort in the mountains of North Carolina, I ran into a woman who noticed the little silver ring I wore on my pinky finger.

"You were a Camp Fire Girl, too!" She exclaimed, and we both made the "sign of the fire" which involves crossing one hand over the other then lifting the right hand, index finger extended in a graceful arch, as we chanted the Camp fire Girl greeting "Wo-Hee-Lo"!

It was great fun. That weekend she and I canoed and reminisced about our separate camp fire experiences while our husbands golfed. No one in her "tribe" had ever gotten a "Ceremonial" dress or finished a headband either. But we agreed, we'd had fun … and we had looked a lot cuter than the Girl Scouts!

The Wonders of Guilt

Some think the intricate art of "guilt-laying" is an acquired skill. Not so!

When I was nine, I went to Camp Robin Hood. I hated camp. It was so organized. I liked to swim, but who wanted ORGANIZED swimming? Popping up in the morning after a shrill blast from some tinny trumpet, then leaping into a lake from whose frigid surface wafted cold, damp mists, was not my idea of fun!

We "Polywogs" (as we were known) practiced our dead-man's float from 7:30 to 8:00 a.m. My skin would just have turned from purple to pale, opalescent blue when … a blast from the "whistle"! Time to get out! Up dead men! Polywogs of the world, arise!

Whistles for swimming! Whistles for lunch! Whistles for singing! I loved to sing, but who wants to sing at the blast of a whistle every day …

particularly when it was summer and the woods and wild flowers called?

My parents MADE me go away to camp. It was really my brother's fault. Dave had gone away to camp every summer for years. The first time he had been nervous about going away from home. I convinced him it would be fabulous fun. He would love it.

I had ulterior motives. I wanted to use his little room for the summer. Dave's room had a metal roof on which the rain played stacatto melodies nights when the moon was out of business and the clouds spilled themselves on our house.

As a result of my *selling* job, Dave went to camp every year until he was too old to be a "camper." After that he became a counselor and continued going to Camp Sequoia every summer leaving me to the cozy cot under the metal roof. Joy!

Then one summer, my parents decided since I'd done such a job of selling David on going to camp, I probably wanted to go myself. HA! Saleswomen don't always buy what they sell.

Before the summer had barely begun, I found myself in a camp with whistles and organized everything plus a bunch of girls who were either:

    a.) wimpier and unhappier than I was, or

    b.) were getting chest bumps and breaking out in hair in strange places, and worse yet,

    c.) were interested in *boys!*

But the worst thing was that it was war-time, and gasoline was rationed.

My father, a salesman, had some gasoline for necessary travel … but no gas for frivolous things like going to the grocery store, or visiting a homesick daughter in a camp in upstate New York.

The other day I came across my solution to the Camp problem. It was a letter, written in pencil from Camp Robin Hood. My mother had saved it all these years. I had wanted to apprise my parents of my feelings … and to plop a little guilt on them.

The letter is the most blatant example of "guilt plopping" I have ever read. I spread guilt with a heavy, unsubtle trowel. The complete, uncensored letter goes as follows:

"Dear Mom, Pop and Berganzolie {my cat},

Well, it's Visitors Sunday. All the parents are with their kids. It was OK up to now, but now all the kids are showing their mothers around. You could of come up on a bus that's what the mothers do. Gee, I no you can't come but it makes ya feel so alone. Most of the kids in camp are eating out with their parents. Oh I miss you so much. I had to be near you and the nearest way was to write. Every few minutes I look up to see if maybe you came. Nancy (my

friend who'd gone with me) feels bad too. Its
alful to hear a mom's or womans voice and not
to have it be yours. There's nothing for me to
do today because everyone is with their mothers
and fathers.

Love Janie"

I didn't get sent to camp after that. My parents couldn't stand it.

Guilt! A wonderful weapon!

Jane Hallock Combs

My Brother, Dave

When I was nine, I hated my brother. He ruined my life. He broke my things. He squashed my caterpillars! He was three years older than I.

Dave was bigger, smarter and always ahead of me! He tried to boss me ... tell me what to do. When and where to do it! Sometimes he "baby sat" with me! I was NOT A BABY! I was nine! I could take care of myself!

When I ran away from home, Dave had been "babysitting" while my parents were out. I was up in our cherry tree conferring with my rag-doll, Mary Ann, when David yanked me down.

"You're not supposed to climb trees! Get down and stay down."

I swung at him with Mary Ann. That's when I realized Mary Ann's leg was still up in the tree.

"You broke my doll!" I lashed out at him again. His arms were longer than mine. He could hold me off easily.

"I'm getting out of here ... and I'm never coming back!" I yelled and stormed into the house, grabbing a peach from the bowl and stamping out the back door to shouts of "Don't be gone long! Mom and Dad will be home soon!"

I'd show him! I was NEVER coming back!

I ran down our hill, and turned onto the Old Hollow Road.

The trees hung down over the road like a dark tunnel. Swell! I found a big rock by the side of the road and sat down to eat my peach and check out the knee which I'd skinned when David yanked me out of the cherry tree. I spit on my knee and cleaned it up some with a crumpled, grey Kleenex from the torn pocket of my old camp shorts. I ate the peach. Sticky peach juice dribbled down my chin. I wiped my face with a dirty hand then pushed back a fugitive strand of straggly hair that

71

had escaped from my wispy pony tail. I was starting to think about heading home when I saw the car. It was cruising down the road with some old guy in it. When it drew up next to me, he leaned out the window and asked me if I knew where a "Susan Matson" lived. I'd never heard of her...

"That's too bad. I wanted to take her picture for a beautiful child contest."

A beautiful child contest! WOW!

Then he was looking at me. He looked at my old tennis shoes with the broken lace ... at my dirty camp shorts ... at my old striped shirt ... at my dirty face with the peach juice all over it. Then he said those *wonderful* words,

"Maybe I could take YOUR picture for the beautiful child contest."

My heart jumped! *My picture in a beautiful child contest!!'*

I ran a dirty hand under my nose. "ALL RIGHT!"

He opened the car door. "Hop in and we'll find a place to take your picture!"

"Never get into a car with a stranger!" My mother's words sounded in my head. Silly words! This man was a *professional photographer!* Wouldn't mother be proud?

But I had been brain washed!

"No! I can't go in a car with someone I don't know!"

"Where does this road go?" He asked

"Oh, just down by the duck pond and out by the ski hill."

"Are there many houses down there?"

"No. There aren't any! There's just the lake, the woods and the hill.

"Well, would it be all right if I drove my car and you walked there? We could meet and you wouldn't have to ride in my car."

That made sense. I said "Sure!"

He drove away and I began to run down the street as fast as I could. When I couldn't see his car anymore. I began to worry, Maybe he remembered where the other girl lived; he'd take HER picture, not mine!

Then I went around a curve and saw his car. The man was standing next to it looking all around.

"Here I am, Mister!" I ran up to him. He had a black bag sitting by his feet.

"What's in the bag?" I asked. "Is that your camera? Can I see it?"

"You'll see it!" He took my hand, "Let's go in the woods and find a good place to take your picture."

As we walked into the woods, I began to feel a little bit nervous. The woods were too dark for a good picture and awfully quiet. I didn't really know this man. What would Mama say?

Halfway up in the woods the man found a big, flat rock. "Sit down."

He was starting to open the black bag. He was nervous, his hands were shaking. I tried to see what kind of camera he had.

As he started to pull something out of the bag I heard my name ... in the distance. Someone calling my name! I knew the voice.

"What's that?" the man asked looking up quickly.

"Oh that's just my big brother!" I said.

With that the man closed his bag fast, grabbed it and started running out of the woods.

I jumped up and ran after him. "Hey, mister!" I screamed, "Wait! You didn't take my picture!"

But he didn't stop. I ran after him ... all the way to the road. I saw him throw his bag into the car, then jump in. He slammed the door and sped off. As he roared away, David came around the corner of the road on his bicycle.

David! He always ruined everything! He'd done it again! I remember I sat by the side of the road and cried for a long time.

Jane Hallock Combs

Big, Bad, Bob

Brothers! They enrich our lives … some more than others.

My friend, Elaine, had three brothers. But they were all younger than she … that hardly counts. It's the BIG brothers in our lives who make such an impact. They also, at least when they are young, tend to stretch the truth a bit. Older, and bigger than their female siblings, they feel they have power. That power can occasionally be absolute. We all know how corruptive power can be … not to mention the corrosive effects of ABSOLUTE power!

MY big brother, Dave, took great joy in misleading me or deliberately leading me astray, like the time he convinced me that the hilly road that led from the bottom of OUR hill was actually the way to heaven. It nearly gave me a heart attack the first day I got on the school bus en route to Kindergarten and the bus headed up that same hilly road to the Dobbs Ferry School. My parents were unsympathetic. I was told not to "be so gullible."

Gullibility is what big brothers rely on, thrive on, feast on.

"Come on, Jane, there's a four-headed cat out in the barn. If you let me have your ice cream cone, I'll show you the cat, I promise." The cone was long gone before we ventured into the barn to see what turned out to be a mother cat with three kittens nursing.

"That's no four headed cat!" I stamped my foot making dust and straw fly. "That's just old Betsy ... she's had babies again!"

Dave wiped the last of the ice cream from the corner of his mouth, then, staying safely out of my range, answered, "Yeah ... but do you see four heads or not? They look pretty attached to me! A four headed cat for sure!"

My best friend, Nancy Cowles, was also blessed with an older brother, Don. We used to exchange big brother horror stories all the time. But we didn't know how easy we had it. In comparison.

I recently ran into an old college friend of mine, an author who writes beautiful, warm, inspiring articles for hunting and fishing magazines. Such an excellent writer and a fine friend, Bob had been a fraternity brother of my brother Dave's. You would never suspect this kind, sensitive man of having been the *champion, rotten big brother* of all time. But he was ... and a very creative one!

As writers do, we were swapping stories about our early childhoods. I told him the one about David, the school bus and the road to heaven. He then admitted to understanding Dave's desire to help me grow up strong and resilient. He had helped his own sister in similar fashion. Bless his heart!

When his little sister, Wendy, started kindergarten, she caused some problems by showing up back at home along about the time her mother was finishing cleaning up the breakfast things. She'd gotten off the bus at school, then headed home on the run.

This happened three mornings in a row before big brother Bob took matters into his own hands.

He grabbed little sister aside and said:

"This is getting serious now, Wendy! I need to talk with you. For three days you've skipped school and come home. Have any of the *Watchers* seen you?"

"*The Watchers?*" Wendy asked as her eyebrows lifted skyward, and her brown eyes threatening to leap from their orbits. "What watchers?"

"You don't know ANYTHING, do you," Bob questioned in classic big brother style.

"At almost every street corner between school and home, there are assigned "watchers" who have little note books. They watch for kids who skip school."

"Then what do they do?"

"When they see you, they write your name down in their little note books. If you try to skip school for the fourth time, one of them will stop you,"

"And..." Wendy was trembling visibly.

"They all carry a very special screw driver which just fits into your belly button. If they catch you skipping school the fourth time, they unscrew your belly button and YOUR LEGS FALL OFF!"

Wendy never skipped school again. Bob was such a help. Big brothers! They're such interesting family members. They enrich our lives. Some more than others, but at times, they do stretch the truth just a teensy bit.

Pirates!

Pirate Eggs are a tradition in my family. I had one this morning. They're great!

A slice of bread with a hole ripped in the middle, the bread popped into a pan with bacon fat or butter (or low fat oil. if you're persnickity!), and then as the bread browns and sizzles, an egg is broken into the middle. Turn it once, and VOILA! A Pirate Egg. Fast, simple, and delicious!

Pirate Eggs are particularly appealing to kids (and most grown ups!) My mother called them "Gypsy eggs," but since my kids didn't know what a "Gypsy" was, I called them "Pirate Eggs."

Things piratical have always fascinated me. I always wanted to *be* a pirate. St. Lawrence University didn't offer a major in piracy though. The closest thing to it was marketing and that just didn't have the same pizazz. I opted for a major in English. That involved writing and I'd been writing stories for years … not actually writing them, but rather telling them to myself. My childhood method for putting myself to sleep was telling myself pirate stories.

I may have been influenced by too many Maureen O'Hara movies, and a love for Errol Flynn didn't *run* in our family … it *galloped.* My elderly grandmother, Mama and I would go together to every movie Errol was ever in. Lots of them involved pirates.

After a particularly exciting one, I remember my grandmother trying to cool herself vigorously with her Jesus fan, saying,

"Well, now *that* certainly got the old blood moving around!"

Grandma was right. There was something about Errol swinging on a ship's halyard, cutlass in hand hollering "Avast ye swabbies … buckle your bilges" or a similar phrase of encouragement. He swung himself across generation gaps with grace ... a paragon of piracy.

My bedtime fantasies were elaborately plotted stories that always featured me as a swashbuckling lady pirate, bracing against the lash of the waves breaking over the bow of my sleek ship as it carried my bloodthirsty crew and me off for another episode of fighting, pillaging and, of course, hot blooded romance.

Naturally, I was always the main character of my stories. I saw myself dressed in knee britches and a ruffly shirt with my waist cinched in by a wide leather belt. (In patterning my outfits after those Maureen O'Hara usually wore, I ignored the fact that my mosquito bitten, cat scratched legs were skinny as sickly twigs, my knees knobby, and I would have looked as glamourous in knee britches as Ichabod Crane. My skimpy blond braids and raggedy bangs didn't bear a whole lot of resemblance to Maureen's lush, hair either ... but imagination needn't dwell too long on realities. With one eye on the mizzen mast, the other on my surly crew, I gripped the rugged wheel and guided my ship on.

Night after night, my gallant, (if a tad bloodthirsty) crew sailed the Spanish Main with me as their bold, beautiful leader, "Lady Jane." The wind and sea spray whipped through my hair and, on alternate nights, either I sank seven Spanish galleons, saving the British Empire from ruin, or was kidnapped from my manor house where I was an aristocratic beauty (knobby knees notwithstanding) and taken aboard a pirate vessel where I would end up not only joining the crew, but becoming their fearless leader. Oh the adventures I had! The stories I could tell!

Telling myself stories always worked like a charm ... put me to sleep every time. Possibly that's why I don't sell more books now. My stories put people to sleep.

Well, watch out you landlubbers. My swash may have buckled a bit, but at heart I'm still a

pirate, so batten down your bilges, and avast you
miserable swabbies!

Big Mike For Dinner

"But the man said they were guaranteed!" Brother Dave spluttered seeing his first business venture at age fifteen going down the drain.

It was wartime. Dave had brought Mike and the others home from New York, carrying them in a box on the train.

"Guaranteed hens," the man had said, "with two or three roosters thrown in for good egg production!"

If two or three roosters make for *good* egg production, our egg productions should have been OUTSTANDING! As it turned out, when those fluffy, yellow chicks dropped their down, we ended up with *twenty five* roosters and five haggard hens, but not many eggs. The hens were too exhausted.

Every morning the roosters would line up on top of their "hen" house and crow their hearts out. Twenty-five roosters welcoming the dawn as if it were an Olympic event is not charming, particularly when the dawn is dawning at 4:30.

"Those roosters have got to go to the block!" said my mother, who was beginning to look as haggard as the hens from lack of sleep. "We're going to have to eat them!"

David and I winced.

"But we can't do that!"

The chickens were all named and all *friends!* From Little Joe, the runt, to Big Mike, king of the roost, they had their personalities. We loved them … noise and all … at least Dave and I did.

But in those war days, meat was hard to come by, so we ate the roosters. Sunday after Sunday, our friends showed up on a platter in the middle of the table.

Since they were Dave's roosters, *he* had to kill them. He swung the axe, his eyes half closed and tears streaming down his face. Big Mike watched it all.

It was almost Thanksgiving, and all the roosters were gone except for Big Mike. Even our pal Little Joe had appeared one day in a pot surrounded by dumplings. David and I filled up on dumplings, but couldn't touch the rest.

The hens had all died, mostly of natural causes, so there was no need to keep Big Mike to help with egg production. Big Mike had watched his companions guillotined, one-by-one, with stupid, stoic calm. He followed Dave around like a trusting dog, tilting his head up as if to say, "That's an awful thing you're doing, but you must have your reasons."

Mike was Dave's particular buddy. He got excited whenever Dave came home from school. He adored Dave. But the order had been given, "Mike must go!"

"Can't we keep him as a pet?" Dave had asked after several futile trips to the chopping block with Big Mike.

"No one keeps a rooster as a pet!" Mom was adamant.

Dave *tried* to kill him. Big Mike didn't resist. He didn't lift his head from the block when Dave put it there. Dave couldn't do it. Three times he tried. Three times he failed.

"It's those big, trusting eyes."

"If you can't do it, Uncle George can!" Mom said.

We were going to Aunt Elsie's and Uncle George's for Thanksgiving dinner. It would be a simple matter to let Uncle George be the executioner. Uncle George HAD been our favorite uncle. How could he do such a dreadful thing?

Thanksgiving dawned cold and clear … and quiet … no Big Mike on the hen house and no joy in our hearts. Dave and I rode in the old Ford to Uncle George's home as to a funeral.

The table was set. The cranberry jelly glimmered red against the white cloth. Little plastic turkeys danced around the cornucopia brinmming with fruit in the middle of the table.

"Bless us, Oh Lord, for these Thy gifts…"

We stood around the table with bowed heads.

Then Aunt Elsie came into the dining room with a platter in her hands and a sheepish look on her face. Dave and I stared at the platter … then at each other.

"Uncle George!" We said together.

On the platter was a small, but distinct meatloaf.

"Where's Big Mike?"

At that moment we heard a jubilant crow coming from the depths of the cellar.

"He's downstairs in the coal bin," offered Aunt Elsie.

"I could have done it," Uncle George said, becoming our favorite uncle again. "I could have done it," he looked embarrassed, "except for those eyes…and he's so trusting…" Dave grinned. I grinned. We dug into the meatloaf. No turkey had ever tasted better!

Jane Hallock Combs

Our Best Thanksgiving

I remember a Thanksgiving when my hand lotion froze solid. I had just turned twelve. My best friend, Nancy, was eleven. We weren't little kids" any more. We were mature "women of the world."

"We're all going upstate to French's for Thanksgiving!"

My mother broke the news while Nancy and I sat warming our hands around steaming cups of hot chocolate with islands of marshmallows floating on top ... We'd just gotten in from ice skating. Our former neighbors, the Frenches, had sold their house on the hill the year before and had bought what was then called a "Motor Court" in upstate New York.

The Frenches had invited all their old neighbors up for the Holiday. There'd be 26 people in all.

"We'll all have cabins," Mama explained. "We'll eat in the big farm house. They'll close the whole motor court to outsiders. It'll just all be the Hill Gang."

Nancy and I groused a little about being away from *our* buddies for the weekend, but then we settled into the serious business of packing.

"It's going to be COLD up there … pack warm stuff," Mama advised. Nancy and I conferred by phone about what we were bringing. The cosmetic case (the one I'd gotten for my birthday) was, of course, of utmost importance.

"I've got my hand cream, my undereye sensitive skin cream and my cuticle oil," I clicked off the litany of my basics. "Then I've got my eyebrow brush, the "Subtle Seal" natural liner, the blue pencil, the make up base, my eyelash curler and six kinds of Tangee lipstick." I was ready.

"Do you think we'd better bring along our nail polish?" Nancy asked. She'd gotten a great little kit from her Aunt Fritzie for *her* last birthday.

"Better to be safe than sorry," I admired her foresight. I threw "Really Raspberry" and "Cotton Candy" into the little side pocket of my Cosmetic case.

It was an eight hour drive from Dobbs Ferry up to the French's place in the Northern Adirondacks. When we hit snow along about Skaneateles I began to wish I had put on my snow pants and worn a sweater under my heavy jacket. Thank goodness for my bunny fur mittens and earmuffs. Maybe warm slacks would have been better than my short, plaid skirt.

Our car heater didn't work. It was COLD! We stopped once while Dad put the chains on the old Ford. "Looks like it's going to be good powder!" Brother Dave lamented the fact that he hadn't been allowed to bring his skis along.

By the time we got to French's, the snow still wasn't much, but as we trudged to the French's farm house, Mama noticed I was wearing my penny loafers and socks ... no boots.

"Jane! Where are your boots!"

"They don't fit over my loafers," I lied. My feet were cold and wet, but I thought I'd better not complain.

We thawed out in front of a pot-bellied stove in the living room.

That night, after our other friends arrived, we all were assigned to little cottages. Nancy and I were sharing a double bed in one little, bitty, VERY cold cottage that had an ancient electric heater we were to turn off before going to bed due to fire hazards.

We had piled blankets on the bed ... but before we climbed in, we both decided we'd better wear our jackets too ... and our mittens. Our brothers (who were sharing the other bed in the cottage) had taken pity on us and lent us their extra pairs of ski socks to wear. It was COLD that night. Probably about -15° outside ... possibly +15° inside.

All I really remember, other than it being VERY COLD that next morning, with knee deep snow, was that when I cracked open my makeup case, which had been stashed under the bed, I found my bottle of Jergens lotion frozen solid!

Nancy and I decided to forego our "beauty" regimen and high tailed it through the snow over to the farm house where we curled up next to the stove and inhaled the aroma of three large turkeys roasting in the big kitchen ovens.

As we sat around the long, noisy tables later with all 26 of our Dobbs Ferry friends ... eating a true Thanksgiving feast ... Nancy and I were thankful for the old galoshes with their flopping hooks Mrs. French had found for us and for the woolly socks from our brothers. Oh, the turkey, the pies, the laughter, the warm feet! What a time!

I can always bring the memories back in a flash with the smell of turkey cooking ... or by looking at any old bottle of Jergens lotion.

Cooking Runs in the Family ... But Not Far Enough!

Cooking is a genetic thing. When people were being encoded for that particular skill, my family's genes were out swimming around somewhere in the gene pool and missed the call. It's sort of too bad, but it has made for some interesting dinner parties.

Cousin Anna Mae used to come to all our family parties. The burning question before every gathering was, "What do you think Anna Mae will bring THIS time?" We always prayed it wasn't "The Cake"!

My stomach was strong. Hallocks genetically HAVE to have strong stomachs, but Anna Mae's cakes were a challenge. Her favorite cake involved some sort of taupe-colored layers covered with magenta frosting decorated with whole dates which looked like huge palmetto bugs crawling all over the cake. Ghastly!

I knew that the cooking thing was hereditary when my daughter called to tell me she had discovered six or seven dried out, old tea bags on her son, Tyson's, window sill.

"What are you doing with these old tea bags," Amy asked.

"I found them in the garbage. They were all wet, so I thought I'd dry them. Mághe likes to have a cup of tea when she comes to visit."

In my grandmotherly role of "Mághe" I appreciated his thoughtfulness, but I have since eschewed tea at my daughter's house. Also cake. I don't eat cake there.

Tyson's sister, Kristie, inherited the same genes.

One afternoon, my daughter opened the refrigerator to find a large, soggy bowl of tired cereal sitting there.

"What's this?"

"It's for Mághe." Kristie said, "she likes cakes. I thought we could use this next time we make one for her."

My grand kids are thoughtful … but the cooking thing is so genetic.

The flaw, indicated by Anna Mae and her cockroachy cakes, comes through my father's line. Anna Mae was my grandmother's cousin. My Grandmother made no bones over preferring painting to cooking.

An artist, Grandma took care of the cooking on Mondays boiling up one huge pot of whatever types of meat Grandpa had purchased for the week: chicken, steak, pork chops. It was all boiled together in lots of water to be served up as individual meals during the rest of the week. Grandma's food wasn't too good, but her paintings were great!

Grandma made all the coffee for the week on Mondays as well. Then it just had to be warmed up every morning. (This before microwave ovens!) By the weekend the coffee was pretty ripe.

Fortunately my Grandfather, father, and uncle were not fussy eaters. Grandma's tutelage didn't help my father or uncle become cooks themselves … though they tried!

My brother, Dave, and I always prayed that Mama would stay well, because we never knew what would happen when Papa cooked. Mama worried a bit too. Particularly after the time she came home to a kitchen where a big pot of something was bubbling furiously on the stove.

"What are you cooking?" she asked my father.

"Onions."

"I don't have any onions!"

"Sure. I found a big sack of them in the garage; they looked pretty dried out so I thought I'd cook them up for you."

"A yellow bag?"

"Yeah, that's the one."

I have to draw back from this sad scene, because my mother loved flowers so, and my father had just cooked up a sack of her prize winning Dahlia bulbs.

Let me defend Papa. He didn't see real well. In fact, his vision was terrible. That's what accounted for the oatmeal episode, I think.

One snowy morning when Mama was in bed "with the pip," Papa outdid himself. The oatmeal was a sodden mess Oliver Twist would have refused. The lumps had lumps. It was tasteless, uneatable. Gross! But eat it Dave and I did with groaning, moaning and loud complaints. Even Dad had to admit it was a "little flat," but he insisted we eat every bit of it, as he did himself.

When we finished, David and I lodged our official complaints with our Mother. Dad came to defend himself from our attacks.

"I followed the directions on the box. It must have been bad oatmeal."

"But I don't HAVE any oatmeal," Mama commented.

"Sure you do. There was a whole box full. I followed the directions exactly."

Mama started laughing. "But that wasn't oatmeal ..." she gasped out, "Don't you remember? I keep bread crumbs in an old oatmeal box You fed the kids cooked bread crumbs."

As I mentioned. It's genetic. What can I say?

Want to do lunch?

Time to Remember

Job interviewing involves specific skills none of which I possessed when I graduated from St. Lawrence University light years ago. Most women graduates would head out on the Marriage/Mommy track back then. Why teach them interviewing skills?

I vividly recall the day I stepped out into the business world. I try to block it out, but I can't!

A friend of Papa's had gotten me an appointment with an old friend of his, the Senior Editor of Time Magazine. What an opportunity! What a disaster!

I can see that day now... a sloppy, cold New York day. The streets and sidewalks filled with wet snow turned to gray slush that slopped around my galoshas as I trudged up The Avenue of the Americas toward the Time/Life Building. The wind tugged at my heavy coat and at the knitted head scarf that was mashing down my $5 hairdo. A sudden gust of wind caught me as I opened the door to the TIME/LIFE lobby launching me half way across the room to the receptionist's desk.

"May I help you?" the surprised woman asked as I stood there, my boots dripping dark slush on the floor.

"I've got an appointment with Mr. "Whatever His Name was" (THAT I've blotted from my memory.)

The receptionist gave me a strange look then suggested I leave my coat and things with her. I knew the first rule taught New York children: "Never let your coat out of your sight! Not in *The City*." I declined her offer, following instead her directions up to the executive suite.

As I threaded my way down the carpeted halls looking for the right office, I became aware my galoshes (which covered my new, gray, suede high heels) were laying a trail behind me somewhat like the one a slug leaves on cement in the summer. I realized too that it was senseless wearing my new gray knit suit then accessorizing it with a brown overcoat, green knitted head scarf and black galoshes (hiding the gray high heels.) When I pulled off the head scarf, my five dollar hairdo, which had included a half gallon of hair spray, was glued firmly to my head like a helmet with small blond hunks sticking out like twigs on a forsythia bush. Lovely!

The Editor's secretary ambushed me before I could plow into his office, and she too offered to relieve me of my outer garments. But, I figured, I'd come this far; I didn't want to have my things stolen, then have to trudge back to Grand Central Station in my knit suit. I refused her offer. I was savvy!

I noticed the secretary's eyebrows raised as she ushered me into the office of the Senior Editor.

After the "hellos", I settled myself into a chair across from the Editor's. I put my purse down, piled my knit scarf on top of it, then unbuttoned my coat. I didn't know what to expect, but I was certain he'd ask questions. I'd answer them. I could do that!

What he said was unexpected.

"Tell me about yourself!"

What could I say?

I remembered admonitions about the need for modesty and humility … I didn't want to brag about my academic achievements (which were super) … I'd go with modesty.

"Well, I like to write a little," I stammered.

"I assumed you did or you wouldn't be here." The Editor said, sounding growly. "Show me some of your work."

"Gee, I didn't bring anything with me." It was such a nasty day and I didn't want my stories to be blown all around New York. Of course, I could have put them in a folder, but I already had my purse to carry …

He asked: "How am I supposed to know you can write?"

"Well, every body says I can." I murmured and lowering my eyes humbly, "And I won the best short story award at St. Lawrence …"

"Do you at least have THAT story with you?"

"No," I said, "but everyone liked it."

"Well, good for them!" he said, getting up from behind the desk, "I don't believe we have any openings now…"

I gathered up my purse and scarf, got up, noticing the little dirty puddle my boots had made on the gold Persian carpet. As he walked me to the door the editor said:

"You don't know much about interviewing, do you?"

As I shook my head, feeling the sticky, hair-matted helmet wobble, the editor said:

"Next time you have an interview, remember to bring samples of your work!...And you'd better be ready to toot your own horn, because if YOU don't do it, nobody will do it FOR you." He opened the door saying:

"AND for HEAVEN'S SAKE, next time give the secretary your blasted coat and boots!"

Jane Hallock Combs

How Do You Say IBM in French?

Back in the Dark Ages when I graduated from St. Lawrence University with a degree in English (minors in Spanish and Psychology), I wasn't equipped to do much of anything. I did write cute doggerel, but there wasn't a big market, let alone a large hue and cry for writers of "cute doggerel," so I did the next best thing. I applied for a secretarial job at IBM International Headquarters on 6th Ave in Manhattan.

The job I applied for was that of secretary to the only (at that time) female Vice President at IBM. I secured the job by my dauntless interviewing skills (I'd worked on them since the debacle with the TIME editor) ... and my strong ability to equivocate.

"Do you know any French," Miss 'Whatever was her name' asked.

"Mais oui," I spouted with practically flawless accent the only phrase of which I was absolutely certain. My two years of high school French had been effectivly drowned out by eight years of Spanish plus a Spanish speaking roommate whose country I had visited on two, lovely, Spanish-filled occasions. Not good for the French language.

But, back to the interview.

"Can you write in French?" I was being asked.

"OH! Mais oui, Mademoiselle."

My favorite song back in those distant days was a number called "Mam'selle." I could pronounce that with as much fluency as I could spout out, "Mais oui!"

But the important thing was ... I got the job! My first post University position ... with IBM INTERNATIONAL! WOW! Big stuff!

The first day on the job was a reality check.

About five minutes into my work, I discovered that my main function in that exciting, new position was to take dictation from Miss What's her name ... in ENGLISH, then to translate said letters into French and mail them off to the IBM office in PARIS. Hum-m-m.

At my lunch break, I rushed off to the nearest bookstore, a dusty, place smelling of milldew and dark with mouse droppings. I found a large, dog-eared French dictionary in my price range (about 50 cents). I whipped back to the office and propped up the dictionary on my desk within an arm's reach of my (what else?) IBM Selectric.

From then on, the job was a piece of cake! I could take dictation pretty well, (occasionally I could even read it back after I took it) ... then I would just settle in at the typewriter with the dictionary propped open and translate like a whiz!

One of the kind things about my situation was that I was the only "French Expert" in the place. No one ... but NO ONE ... ever saw the letters which went whipping out of the New York Office to swoop across the ocean to somewhere in Pareé. I always thought that was a little negligent on IBM's part. But I wasn't about to say so!

Anyway, angels do watch over us mortals. not that we're always worth the effort. So all went well for about three months. Then my boss, whose name my memory has deleted, came into my cubicle smiles all over her face, speaking those fateful words:

"Next Tuesday, Monsieur Bouchard from the French office is coming over for a meeting. He's anxious to meet you!"

I was pretty anxious too!

Tuesday, unfortunately, arrived as did Monsieur Bouchard despite my prayers to the contrary.

Ms. Whoosis brought him back into my little corner of the world, made the introductions, then stood back waiting for a torrent of fluent, mellifluous French to float forth and in general to "let ze good times r-roll."

I stuck out my hand, cranked up my mouth to fit around the words and said, "Bon-gour Ma-sieur."

Monsieur Bouchard took my hand and, French gentleman that he was, touched it for an instant to his lips. He looked up with his Gallic eyes twinkling as he ended my translating career with the words, "SO…you are ze Lady zat writes ze *funny, funny* letters!"

PART 2

"Pst Kid! Ya Want Some Hot Salami"

Serving Time in the Cooler

I usually tip well in restaurants. I have great empathy with table servers.

I was a waitress once in Florida. Actually I was a "Lobster Girl." We were all called that at "Lobster Heaven." We looked cute in our mariner uniforms with the jaunty sailor hats. Well, most of the waitresses looked cute. I just looked harried.

It wasn't the actual serving of food that bothered me, it was more the time I spent locked in the walk-in cooler. It was cold in there, and I was always afraid no one would find me until I looked like one of those frozen Indian mummies up in the Andes.

It was tricky going into the cooler to get cream or whatever it was I needed, carrying a tray in one hand, trying to keep my hat from sliding off my head, and propping the door open with one foot. The foot need only slip an instant and there was the dull thud of the door slamming behind me. Then I would be nestled up next to twenty boxes of frozen shrimp, eighteen gallons of cream and a bunch of dead meat I didn't want to get to know personally.

I'd bang on the door and holler my head off. Eventually some kind hearted bus boy would open the door and answer the manager who wanted to know *what in the world all the noise was about*! The bus boy would say it was "Just that dumb waitress who keeps locking herself in the cooler!"

I'd bluely slink out of cooler-land and go on my way serving food some of which would find its way to the floor before I got out of the kitchen.

I remember a man asking me, "How come my friend got twelve popcorn shrimp, and three hushpuppies, while I got three shrimp and nine hushpuppies?" (If I'd notice a plate was a little on the light side before I left the kitchen, I'd always throw on a few more hushpuppies to even things up.)

Some of my fellow workers told me, "If you drop something, just pick it up, and put it back on the plate. No one will know the difference." It made me gag. So I just went on leaving food in my wake while tossing hushpuppies around to even things up.

My tips weren't great. Usually with good reason! One day, though, I thought I had it made. A family party came in with an elderly lady, all her sons, daughters, and something like fifteen head of kids. Twenty five people in all! Wooh! I thought. Big tip time!

I spent forever with them as the kids slopped and spilled everything slop-able or spillable. I ran back and forth to the kitchen supplying their every need while trying to balance my hat and my tray both of which were constantly in danger.

I had no time for my other tables (given to other servers since I was so tied up with my big group). Twenty seven trips back and forth for Cokes, extra napkins, helping a mother crawl under the table to retrieve her two year old ... not a fun time ... especially since said two year old kept hitting me on the head with her soup spoon. (I only suffered one short lock in in the cooler though! I was proud!)

At last it came to an end! As I stood watching with my "lobster girl" hat askew and my stained apron hanging at an oblique angle from where one of the kids had tried to use it as a handkerchief, they all got up and began to leave.

As they headed towards the door, the dear, old grandmother bustled up close to me and whispered:

"There's something for you, dear! In the middle of the table!"

Whoopee! It had taken me forever serving that crowd, and watching me had finally convinced the manager of my total ineptitude as a waitress

... but I had my reward. There in the middle of the table was a crisp, new, one dollar bill!

The next day, the manager said he thought I didn't really have the makings of a waitress. I believe I kissed his feet and danced out of there singing.

But, I have always appreciated servers and try to leave nice tips.

Oh ... and if ever I ever hear a distant pounding when I am eating, I ask, "Do you happen to have a waitress in your cooler?"

Accidental Teacher

I never intended to teach. It was all an insidious accident.

There was a beautiful day when I finally had all three of my kids in school. My life had simmered down to a lovely, ordered routine that involved mornings full of flowers and coffee, a modicum of housework and a cozy rendezvous with my typewriter from 10:00 till 2:00. I wanted to be a WRITER! I'd been yearning for that for years ... at last it had happened ... Joy, joy! I'd actually sold my first three stories. I was *on my way!!*

Then I made a classic mistake. I volunteered to be a "class mother." It sounded so innocuous. What did a class mother do, anyway? Make a few cupcakes, go to a couple of class parties, maybe drive a carload full of little darlings to the zoo on occasion. Amy's second grade class needed a "Mother." Amy used tears. I'm a sucker for tears.

The next week was Halloween. Amy's teacher asked me to fix cupcakes for the party and bring a little Kool-aid. That I could DO. I was to be there at 1:00 sharp to drop off my "goodies" (The teacher had obviously never tasted my cooking). I could stay for the party if I wanted, or make myself scarce coming back later for the "clean up." PIECE OF CAKE!

At 1:00 p.m. on Halloween I showed up ... arms full of ghoolish cupcakes, Koolaide and BLACK napkins.

I opened the door to room 212 and thought I was at the zoo. The snake pit to be exact. There were kids milling all around the room, standing on desks, crawling around the floor, engaged in all kinds of mayhem.

Behind the desk in the corner cringed, not Amy's teacher (a lady with great control), but an ancient, elderly person with a pained expression on her tired, wrinkled face.

I entered the room, dodging a spit ball the size of a pumpkin, and said, "Where's Miss Jones?"

"She's sick today," a feeble voice croaked out at me. "I'm the substitute." Then her eyes took on a *unnatural* gleam ... She smiled, a crooked, smile straight from "Friday the Thirteenth #32."

"Are you the Class Mother?"

I muttered something affirmative as an eraser hurled past my ear.

"Would you mind running the party? I'm a little old for this, and my arthritis is kicking up today." She screwed her face up into what could pass as a painful smile.

Well, I was no teacher, but I did have three kids, plus a menagerie of other animals at home. I took over. I peeled eight kids off the wall, confiscated all lethal weapons and threw out some magic words.

"Party time! Cupcakes, KOOL-AID ... CANDY... when everyone is sitting in his or her own seat and is QUIET!"

It worked. I passed out the goodies, read a story, organized a small game, sang three songs with them, and it was bus time. While watching the last of the kids climb on the bus, I spoke with a couple of teachers who were also doing "bus duty."

"Who IS that old lady in 212, substituting for Miss Jones?" I asked.

She was the only substitute around! When a teacher was sick it was either the ANCIENT ONE or no one.

"Lots of times," one teacher said, "We don't have ANY sub. We just take turns peeking into the classroom to see they're not killing each other.

Oh my Lord! This was the school MY children were in! I couldn't stand it. The next day I called the principal and volunteered to substitute. I wasn't a teacher, but I did have a B.A. (I had discovered that the ancient one didn't even have any kind of degree!)

"I could substitute if you were really in a pinch," I volunteered. Silly me. Principals are ALWAYS in some kind of pinch.

"Would you teach kindergarten, full time?" She asked.

"You're kidding!" I gasped. "My degree is in English. *I'm a writer!* I've never taken an education course in my life. I couldn't do that! I DON'T WANT TO DO THAT!"

They were short one kindergarten teacher. Big teacher shortage. They were desperate. *Obviously!*

"You could just 'substitute' until we get one!" I was too young to know how devious principals can be.

"It's your son Greg's class. The teacher's moving to North Dakota." I could picture the ancient ONE trying to take care of a bunch of kindergarteners…not to mention … *MY GREGORY!*

"Well maybe just until you get someone…"

I didn't KNOW how addictive teaching could be. Twenty-two years later I was still teaching and still muttering:

"Well, MAYBE FOR just one more little semester…"

I Used to Smell

I've always loved the smell of a school. Especially an old school, a school redolent with with the fragrance of many children, rich with aromas of years of tears, laughter, joys, and sorrows, flavored with the salty smell of old gym shoes and sweaty socks. You know the smell. Unlike any other.

It made me feel warm and comfortable the first time I went into the Rochester Adult Center and climbed up the wide, creaking wooden stairs with the worn handrails to begin my Adult Education teaching career. It was a smell that had good associations for me. That was back when I could smell.

When I fractured my skull, my sense of smell went west. Let me tell you about it.

My husband Bill was putting together a desk for our first computer. You know the kind, made of pressed wood with a slick, shiny surface. Not too expensive but looks good and does the job.

Bill was working on it in the garage on a hot, Florida, summer day. I was in a 'good-wife mode' and took pity on my sweaty, cussing husband who was making great noises in the garage flinging skyward imprecations of what he thought of the blinking idiots who wrote directions for putting things together.

I fixed Bill a glass of iced tea. Tea, not music, soothed *my* savage beast. I brought it to him tip-toeing carefully through the chaos of the garage where desk parts lay scattered around like tornado debris.

Several slick, shiny boards rested atop one another waiting their turn to be pegged into the slowly assembling desk.

To reach Bill with the tea, I needed to step on those boards. When my foot touched the top one it was as though I had hopped on a skate board … a jet propelled skate board. It flew out from under me as the iced tea went in a million directions Up with the feet, down with the tea, and crack with my head on the cement floor. (A lot like an egg cracking, really. Not nice.) I thought I was going to die there on the garage floor surrounded by desk parts, tea-ice and our entire neighborhood which had heard the crash and come stretching their necks to see.

I didn't die, though there were times I wished I would. The skull had fractured slightly. Just slightly, but enough to lay me up for several weeks glugging water with pain killers while listening to Beethoven's Violin Concerto (over and over) as I lay prone on the couch with a cat on my stomach.

I didn't have any bad effects from my skull fracture, other than I couldn't bear to crack eggs for a while, and I swore never again to bring Bill tea, but I did lose my sense of smell. Oh, I can occasionally smell extremely strong odors like amonia held directly under my nose, but your everyday rose sniffing is out. It doesn't usually bother me.

At the time, I was teaching adult foreign students. We always had a pot of coffee and cups in the front of the classroom. One day, an Israeli student brought some of his nation's coffee for us to try. He opened the bag, held it under my nose saying, "Just smell it, Ms. Combs, isn't it WONDERFUL!"

"I'm sure it's just great, Ibrahim," I told him, then proceeded to explain my loss of smell. Ibrahim was very sympathetic. His dark eyes welled up with sadness for me.

"But I'll enjoy *drinking* the coffee", I assured him.

We fixed the strong, black, Israeli coffee. A nice change from the supermarket "El Cheapo" brand we'd been using. Everyone talked about it during their coffee break. Then back to work.

As I walked around the room checking the individual progress of my students, I overheard

Ibrahim talking to his neighbor. He had glanced at me, and looking horribly sad, scrooched up his dark eyes saying:

"You know, Shem, our teacher doesn't smell good!"

H-m-m-m!

He may have been right, but before word got around the class, I decided we'd better do a little work on adverbs!

The Tooth Fairy and the Nazis

My son, Greg, was a strange kid. I remember when he lost his first baby tooth. As we tucked the tiny, white incisor beneath his pillow, I told him the wondrous story about the tooth fairy who would waft into his room sometime during the night, slip the little tooth out from its hiding place and leave in its stead *money!* Maybe a quarter, maybe fifty cents ... but cold hard *CASH!*

Greg seemed awfully quiet about it. Maybe he was just in "awe"!

A little later, I walked by my son's room to find him sitting cross legged just inside his doorway with his baseball bat cradled across his lap.

"Greg!" I exclaimed. "What's with the baseball bat?"

My son looked up at me, brown eyes serious and intent.

"No fairy's coming into MY room while I'm sleeping!"

He planned to bonk the poor, long suffering tooth fairy on the head and send her away.

There was no mollifying Greg, so I ended up Scotch Taping a note to his door informing the tooth fairy she could find the tooth on the kitchen table and to please leave the loot there as well.

I should have known. That sort of thing runs in our family. Few people today know about how cousin Anna Mae and Ezra saved Westchester county from the Nazi invasion. It's a grim story, but one that should be told.

My grandmother's cousins, Anna Mae and Ezra, lived in what once was a huge old farmhouse in Chappaqua, N.Y. It had been something of a showplace before Anna Mae and Ezra's parents died, and Anna Mae and Ezra went dippy.

It wasn't so huge and certainly not a showplace when I first saw the house. By then

Anna Mae and Ezra had finished tearing off ten or twelve rooms looking for the "pot of gold" that was supposedly hidden behind one of the walls. It was exciting walking around the house. You had to take care though, because sometimes a stairway would lead up to a room that was no longer there. Occasionally you would open a door to look out at a corn field twenty feet below.

"You ought to at least seal that stairway off," my dad would say. "Somebody's going to get hurt."

There was no electricity in the house, and the flickering oil lamps made the place really spooky at night with the walls deep with shadows. I remember wandering through rooms filled with piles of old mildewing newspapers, dusty antiques and stacks of canned goods … mostly cat food. Anna Mae and Ezra always had lots of cats scampering around doing unmentionable things in all sorts of places. The house had an intriguing odor about it.

It had an abandoned look too, possibly because of all the peeling paint and the shutters hanging at interesting angles near the windows and the doors of the second floor leading to nowhere.

It wasn't surprising to the rest of the family that vagrants had broken into the house one night when Anna Mae and Ezra were out. Who would have thought anyone would LIVE there!

Anna Mae and Ezra came home to find the door open and the cats running distractedly around, while empty dust circles on the floor marked where some of the piles of canned goods had been.

"It had to be Nazi spies," Ezra decided. "They're looking for a good hideout ... a place that could be a perfect control center when the rest of the Nazis arrive."

From that night on, Anna Mae and Ezra refused to sleep in their house. Instead, they drove to Harmon Station, thirty miles away in their rickety, old, green Plymouth.

Ezra had "served in WW I" but had been felled by a case of the measles and never gone overseas. However, he'd *been a soldier.* This was his chance to serve. He felt certain if an attack came, it would be by train. Somehow Nazi troops would board the Hudson line of the New York Central (presumably at Grand Central Station) and then roar up the railroad line to disembark at Harmon and attack Westchester. It wouldn't have been a good military operation, I'm afraid, not well thought out, but Ezra was prepared.

Every night at dusk, Ezra would don his WW I uniform, and pack Anna Mae into the car along with his trusty baseball bat. They drove to Harmon Station, picked a good lookout spot where they could see the trains arriving from New York, and then, with Ezra's baseball bat across his knees, he and Anna Mae spent the sleepless nights waiting to bash arriving Nazis.

They did this for MONTHS! And it obviously worked. Word about the Harmon Defense Team must have leaked out ... because the Nazis NEVER did attack Westchester. All thanks to my Grandmother's cousins, Anna Mae and Ezra.

So my son Greg's defense against the tooth fairy came naturally, I guess.

Poor Little Boy With a Broken Leg!

The year my son, Greg, broke his leg, my husband and I had been loyal laundromat customers. We'd cooperated on the job. Husband would drop the stuff in the coin washer on his way to work and a little later, I'd run by to put it in the dryer. Four year old Greg LIKED TO HELP. He was a sturdy little guy with great determination ... usually a help. Not always.

One day, while trying to "fly like superman", Greg had launched himself out of the upper window of our neighbor's barn. Superman he wasn't. Greg he was. He'd landed on a stone wall. Fortunately his fall was deflected by the branch of a tree so he didn't land on his head, but he did break his leg spectacularly. The neighbor who picked him up compounded the insult and the fracture. As a result, Greg spent weeks in the hospital in traction. Terribly traumatic for everyone, especially Greg.

When he finally came home, Greg had a double cast on his legs ... from waist to the knee on his good leg and waist to toes on his broken one (with a bar running between the two legs for rigidity ... and, I think, for help picking up a heavy four year old plus cast).

By the time he was due to get the cast off, Greg was pretty antsy. True, I'd taken him for lots of walks in an old carriage-stroller with his casted legs sticking out like prongs of a snow plow in front of us, but this was a boy who liked to *move around and check things out*. In the house, Greg could get around pretty well. He'd learned to drag himself along the floor using his arms to pull his plump self along (while his plaster coated legs scraped behind leaving permanent scars in the soft, pine floors). You could hear him scraping his way through the house.

Greg was nothing if not resourceful. He found it great fun to scream "Help! Help!" when he was lying safe on the downstairs couch. He liked to see how fast someone could come to his aid. I clocked in at a 30 second stair descent before I caught on to his game. If he'd had the cast on much longer, I could have qualified for the Olympic Stair Dash team.

The day before his cast was due to come off ... my husband dropped the laundry off at the laundromat on the way to work. I said I'd take Greg on an outing with me while I did the "drying" part of the laundry. I piled Greg and myself into my little white Volkswagen (with the sunroof) and headed to town. Nice outing for Greg.

When I got there, I told Greg I just had to pop the clothes in the dryer ... stick in a couple of quarters and I'd be back to drive him on an exciting tour of downtown Putnam while the clothes dried. Who knows ... we might even pass an ice cream parlor where I could pop for some cones. Who could tell?

I'd just piled the clothes in the dryer when someone said: "Well, look at THAT!" I heard a familiar 'scrape, scrape' sound.

I looked out the laundromat window. There was Greg who had somehow opened the Volkswagen door, gotten out of the car, and was dragging himself down the sidewalk on his stomach heading for the laundromat.

I rushed outside, picked him up and deposited him back in the Volkswagen.

"Honey, Mommy'll be right back! Let me put the laundry in the machine. It'll only take a minute. Then we'll go get ice-cream."

Back to the laundromat and a repeat of the previous episode. Gregarious Greg hated to be left alone for a minute.

"Scrape, scrape, scrape." Back he came down the sidewalk.

"I hep you, Mommy!" He smiled his huge smile.

Back again to the Volkswagen.

"Sweetie," I tucked him into his seat, gave him his teddy bear, a book and a hug. "Tomorrow your cast comes off, and then you can move around! Now you have to wait for me for one little minute!"

I made sure the sunroof was open, then I LOCKED the car doors.

I ran into the laundromat, finished shoving the clothes in, slammed the door then shot quarters into it as quickly as I could. *Not quick enough!*

By the time I got outside there was a little crowd around the white Volkswagon. My plump little boy had pulled himself up and was leaning out the sunroof making a speech:

"Ladies and gennulmen! I'm a poor little boy with a broken leg! My mommy locked me in the Volkswagen. I don't think it's nice to lock a poor little boy with a broken leg in a Volkswagon. I was only trying to HEP!"

I heard nasty comments as I pushed through the surly crowd, unlocked the car, got in and sped away. Greg heard a couple of nasty comments, too. From a surly mother. Something about breaking his other leg, I think. Did I stop for ice-cream? I don't remember. Probably. I was always a sucker for any poor little boy with a broken leg who was "only trying to hep his mommy."

Jane Hallock Combs

Robin/Manfred/Indian Friend/Bird Girl

A pair of industrious wrens working on a nest in our new bird house reminded me of my daughter, Robin, who spent part of one year as a bird.

It was the summer she changed her name from Robin to Manfred. Her complete adopted name was "Mighty Manfred the Wonder Dog" after her favorite cartoon character. She talked everyone in our neighborhood into calling her either "Mighty Manfred," or "Manfred." Even the adults called her that. We got used to it after a while.

Robin/Manfred, was three that year. An imaginative child who populated our home with an entire tribe of Indians with whom she would play, holding invisible hands and occasionally bursting into war dances complete with whoopings and war chants. I didn't object to the Indians. They were mostly friendly. It was a problem only if you started to sit down in a chair already occupied by 'an Indian' or leaned over to kiss your child good night and found your hand smack in the middle of an Indian's face. Unnerving!.

As the weather that year warmed up, Robin/Manfred and the Indians played outside more. One day I found her picking up handfuls of new mown grass and making little piles of it in the lower branches of our young fruit trees.

"What are you doing with the grass?" I asked.

"Making bird's nests." Robin/Manfred barely paused in her work.

"That's really nice," I said hating to discourage her creativity. "But birds like making their OWN nests."

"Now they don't *have* to," she said grinning. "I've got the nests all ready."

145

She was right. I could see grassy nests in all the lower limbs of our trees. Not too tidy ... but nests there were.

"Here birdy, birdy!" my little tow-haired, Indian/Manfred called, squatting on the lawn next to a grass-laden tree. "Come-on, birdy, birdy.

"Honey," I told her, "birds aren't going to come to your nests. "They'll be afraid if they see a little girl here. They won't know you're their friend. Why don't you (and the Indians) come inside. We'll make some cookies."

While I made cookies, Robin disappeared into her room. I could hear the snip, snip of her little, blue scissors and the rustle of paper.

By the time I had finished taking the last of the cookies from the oven, my daughter came to me with an armful of cut-up, construction paper.

She had yellow, pointed pieces of construction paper under all her fingernails and a large yellow triangle in her mouth ... pointed side sticking out.

146

"What on earth are you doing?" I almost dropped the tray of cookies.

She had trouble talking around the thing in her mouth.

"I've been making a 'bird thuit'. Would you tie my 'wingth' on?" She handed me the big, red, paper wings she carried in her yellow trimmed hands.

"If I look like a bird, I won't scart thum." I tied the paper wings around her arms, and then helped her attach her "tail" to the back of her jeans. I watched in fascination as Robin/ Manfred/Indian Friend/Bird-girl waddled out the back door.

A MINUTE later I stepped out to watch as she squatted on the ground near a tree calling invitingly, "Cheep-cheep, Cheep cheep!"

Robin often influenced other children in the neighborhood. When the kids found out the reasons behind her masquerade they pestered their own mothers for "bird suits."

Before you knew it, there were a half dozen little kids dressed in paper "bird suits" sitting out under our grass-filled fruit trees. They all chorused "Peep-Peep," "Cheep Cheep" or a variation thereof. Our house sounded like the bird house in the zoo on a bad day.

The real birds never came. They probably looked at all the kids in bird suits and went to Kansas. I think the Indians went with them. They disappeared about the same time.

The day Robin stopped being "Mighty Manfred", I remember well. She had been playing in her sand box when her best friend, Robert, came to join her.

"Hi, Manfred!" Robert greeted her.

Robin/Manfred said nothing.

"Hi, Mighty Manfred!" Robert was getting formal.

Nothing.

"Hi, Mighty Manfred the Wonder Dog!" Robert practically shouted in her ear.

Robin looked quizzically up at Robert and said in a voice full of serious, childhood reality:

"My name is not Manfred, it's Robin." And it was from then on. Our lives continued. Life is good, but sometimes I see an old cartoon on television … and I yearn for of my own Mighty Manfred, friend of Indians … and a little girl in a bird suit.

Taking the Offensive in the Market

(or …I never saw that kid before in my life!)

When grocery shopping with small boys, it's wise to remember that the best defence is an offense! It's no use hiding by the meat counter trying to look like pale liver while:

    a. the burglar alarm is blaring,

    b. the manager is rushing around shouting obscenities,

    c. your son has slipped the hammerlock you try to keep on him at all times and … is no where to be seen.

You must be aggressive! I always shout:

"It must have been that kid who's been careening around here with the sword he filtched from the toy section!" I point down the nearest aisle, "the last I saw of him, he was screaming 'Banzai' and had just knocked down three old ladies, a display of tuna fish and a dyspeptic potted plant!"

I always lead the attack!

"You go down aisle eight! I'll head him off at the cat food!"

I sprint down the pet food aisle. Opposite the rear door, I execute a quick side step, and there I am … outside in the parking lot! It saves a lot of wear and tear on the nerves and on my multitudinous guilt complexes.

Denying the kid is a good gambit too. It's hard to deny him when he's sitting in your shopping cart dive bombing jars of jelly on the floor, but when he's off and running, you can just nudge people and say:

"See that kid?"

"The one peeling all the stickers off the bananas?"

"Yeah, disgraceful the way some people…"

It's only when you're lulled into a state of calm that you encounter danger in the market. Like the day I was rummaging through the rutabagas, and Gregory came up slipping his

151

hand through one of mine and smiling his gorgeous smile. We continued through the store … hand in hand.

The manager came up to me.

"Is this your little boy?" I suppressed my natural reaction, clutched my son to my side and murmured: "Oh yes!"

"Pretty quiet now, aren't you?" the manager said, "It must have scared you!"

"What scared him," I asked, instantly on the alert.

"The noise when the window fell in."

"What window fell in?"

"The front window."

"What front window?" I asked, sounding redundant.

"The one he pushed the shopping cart into."

"Impossible!" I shouted. "We're just passing through. It must have been that kid who's been careening around here with a sword. You go down Aisle eight. We'll head him off at the cat food!"

We're very offensive in the market.

Jane Hallock Combs

Antimacassars and Dangerous Boys

Back in the days when men used to slother their hair with a greasy mess called *macassar,* women spent a lot of time crocheting little things called "antimacassars" which they draped on chairs and couches to preserve the upholstery from said greasy mess. My grandmother's house was festooned with "antimacassars"... as was Marion Howard's.

The Howards were our older, childless next door neighbors when we lived in Connecticut. Last month I visited the old home town discovering that Marian Howard still lived there. I stopped by to see her, but she wasn't home. I peeked in the windows though, and saw the antimacassars all still in place on the overstuffed chairs. It brought back a flood of memories

I remembered my years of living with three active children next door to Marian's house. Life with children isn't easy, but it's never dull. There's always the question of what's going to happen next.

When Gregory, my own Bete Noir, was four, I lived in a constant state of anticipation. It wasn't so much the things that he accomplished like setting the fire in back of the post office or getting expelled from summer Bible camp for doing a belly dance with a raisin in his navel … it was the "possibilities." It was like living with a bomb likely to go off at any moment. Greg's mouth knew nothing of control. His opinions and thoughts spewed out like water pouring through a dam spillway.

The learning disorder which caused a lot of Greg's hyperactivity and unpredictabily involved his auditory sense, which meant he confused many words. I remember the day he asked about the Howards.

"Mommy, why aren't the Howards ever in their store?"

"What do you mean, Sweetie?" I asked. "The Howards don't have a store. They work at Old Sturbridge Village"

"No," Greg was getting riled,"You know their store down town, the Howard Store where you get hammers and nails and stuff!"

Amy who was two years older than Greg and infinitely more sophisticated, loved to help her brother with word problems.

"It's not the Howard Store," she explained." You can say it right. Listen and repeat after me. (Amy's a born teacher)."

She said, "Say 'Hard'"

"Hard," Greg echoed.

"Now say, 'word'."

"Word."

"Now you've got it," said big sister. "The *Hard Word Store*." She smiled. (She may have been a born teacher, but Amy had a couple of problems of her own.)

Worse than misinterpretations of words coming INTO Greg's brain was the problem of what would spew *out* of his mouth in any given situation.

The day I headed out to collect for the heart fund drive and had to take Greg with me, I was nervous. It's always unsettling to walk into someone's house carrying a live hand grenade … especially one with a loose pin. He was only four, yet his opinions were strong and expressed with a loud, rumbly voice that could be heard for three and a half miles.

As soon as we walked into Marian Howard's house and I saw Greg looking around at the old fashioned, overstuffed furniture complete with antimacassars on every arm and headrest coordinating with the delicate lacy doilys under each lamp, knick-nack and ash tray, I knew we were in trouble. Before I could start my heart fund speil, or better yet just dump the information and get the heck out of there, the bomb went off:

Greg's voice boomed out. "Hey! What kind of a house IS THIS?"

I tried to clap a hand over his month. My hand was full of heart fund brochures. He knocked me away. "What do you *CALL* this kind of a house anyway?"

I started backing towards the door, mumbling my appologies when the bomb turned into a magician's bouquet of flowers with Greg's next words:

"It's *BEAUTIFUL!*" My son's face was radiant as he looked around the living room. "This is the *most BEAUTIFUL house I have ever seen!*"

I thought about Greg last month as I peeked into Marian Howard's front window. I'm sorry she wasn't home. She's have asked about Greg. My Bete Noir was always a very special favorite of hers.

Influence in High Places

The summer, Greg, was four, his grandfather died. Greg had adored his grandpa. They'd been friends. He'd love to watch Grandpa Jack work in his shop. The shiny tools and equipment hanging on the walls and sitting gleaming on the shelves fascinated him. He'd sat lots of times singing happily to himself as he watched Grandpa working. Sometimes you could see the two of them sitting by themselves in a quiet place out under the huge oak trees sharing cocoa and doughnuts. They had laughed and talked and understood each other.

They were so much alike. Both of their voices were big and rough. Greg's deep, little boy voice always surprised people. Greg and Grandpa Jack's hearts were big, too … and gentle.

Greg's grandpa was alone when he died. He'd been driving to Cape Cod to meet part of the family who had gone there earlier. He'd had a heart attack as he drove alone on a major highway. He'd managed to pull his car off the road before he died.

We heard the news a short time later. Of course, we all were terribly upset. We drove to Cape Cod that night from Connecticut to break the news to the rest of the family who were in a cottage with no phone. Greg and his sisters had stayed with friends while we were gone.

Children accept death in a different manner from adults. After the first shock, they go on about their lives.

Gregory missed his grandfather, but his sorrow at losing him was eased somewhat by the joy of having many of his grandfather's tools right there in his own father's workshop. Greg could be near them every day as much as he wanted, but, of course, he couldn't use them. What frustration!

He *wanted* to use them! He wanted very much to OWN them himself. He especially wanted to own one large, yellow drill. It was a drill he had watched his grandfather use many times. It had been one of his Grandpa's favorite tools.

"Can I see the big drill, Daddy?" He would ask his father. "Can I hold it? Can I turn it on?"

When the answer was no, and it always was "no" to the last question, Gregory would become angry.

"But Grandpa would want me to have that drill!" He would stamp his small foot. "Grandpa would WANT ME TO HAVE HIS TOOLS!" He would start to cry. Fat tears rolled down plump cheeks. "Grandpa would let me use that drill!" The loss of his grandfather became completely centered on the tools.

One sunny, fall day, Greg came into the kitchen where I was fixing some lunch. I had been by myself and feeling sad. I was happy to have Greg's company. I smiled when I saw him.

"Mommy, is Grandpa really in heaven?" he asked.

"Yes, honey, he is. He really is! We'll all go there ourselves some day. We'll see Grandpa then."

"Mommy," Greg asked, "can Grandpa see me now?"

"Oh, sweetie, *of course he can.*" I was glad that Greg was beginning to express his feelings about his grandfather. He'd been so preoccupied with the tools, I'd been a little worried.

"Can Grandpa hear me too?" my son asked.

"Certainly he can, Honey," I answered. "He can see and hear you as well as I can right now!"

With that, Gregory put his hands on his sturdy four year old hips, raised himself up as tall as he could, and looked up towards the kitchen ceiling. He called out in his booming, little-boy voice so like his grandfather's:

"Grandpa! Can you hear me?" He spoke a little louder. "You know that drill?" He waited a moment. "That big yellow one?" He waited another moment. "Can I HAVE IT?"

There was another brief pause, and then Greg turned to me, his face full of smiles. He'd had the final word from Grandpa himself.

"Grandpa says I can have it!"

Telephonitis

Rumors to the contrary, most women hate the telephone. That is, most women with 1.3 or more children hate the telephone.

Let the house be as silent as a sarcophagus, with the children and animals scattered to the four winds; you tippy-toe to the phone to call your best friend, and immediately from out the cracks in the wall come the children, screaming and hitting each other, just exactly one half foot beyond your reach. Something about the tingle of the wires attracts the darlings magnetically. Not to mention the dog who normally ignores you but now wants to climb on your lap (the fact that he weighs 80 pounds and has a terminal case of fleas has no bearing on the matter.)

This is all bad enough, but let the phone ring (usually just before supper, when the Pizza Supreme has started to burn, and the washing machine has begun a banging break-dance in time to the radio which some kid has turned UP full blast) and the conversation goes something like this:

"Hello dear, this is great Aunt Sarah. I'm knitting..."

"Robin, turn that thing down, I'm on the phone with someone. WHO IS THIS?" I scream into the receiver while I stretch my leg out and try to turn off the oven with my big toe.

"Great-Aunt Sarah, dear, and I wanted to know what size..."

Amy and Greg roll across the floor gouging eyes over who gets to sit in the captain's chair for dinner. I make a swipe at them and drop the phone.

"Sorry, Aunt Sarah, you were saying?"

Robin holds a sign up for me to read: "*Can I have one? Amy did.*"

I make a face at them then turn back to the phone.

"Dear, I'm making a sweater for…" I can barely see the washing machine dancing away from the wall through the smoke from the burning pizza.

"That's lovely, Aunt Sarah…*wait till I get my hands on you!*"

Amy and Robin are now rolling on the floor screaming,"You had the last…"

"No I didn't YOU did!"

"What's that, dear?" My aunt asks. She sounds confused. Poor dear. Getting old I guess.

Greg points to something that has happened behind the rocking chair. Holding his nose, he mouths words so that he won't disturb me. The cat is pussyfooting across the room.

"Get that cat," I shout, "and put her OUT! Now what was it, Aunt Sarah, you wanted a sweater size?"

"Never mind, dear, I'll make it for Nancy's boy."

I miss out on more darn sweaters!

Backlash in the Stomach

Complaints about my Thursday night suppers make me sick! Just because I run out of food along about mid Thursday and have to improvise a bit does not mean I am a rotten cook ... just an ingenious one. Take the other night...

I was rooting around through my recipes looking for something I could whip up with two spotted peaches, an unripened avocado, one cup of sour sherry, four eggs and an antique can of Chinese noodles. That eliminated "Ours Au Grand Veneur" right there! I was clean out of bear loin, besides ... you have to marinate it for four to five days, and the kids were getting hungry.

"Why don't we go the MacDonald's?" Suggested Amy.

"Here's a recipe in <u>Calculated Risks</u>," I said, leafing through my favorite cookbook.

"*Eggs Diana a la Scrofula*"... I can grate the avocado and use it in place of the Provolone!"

"How about MacDonald's?" asked Robin, a charter member of the Thursday night 'Coward's Club'.

"What about *Crab Spaghetti Luigi?*" I asked. "Only we'll use hard cooked eggs instead of crabmeat and the Chinese noodles in place of the spaghetti. That should be a taste treat!" I noticed the cat quietly retching in the corner.

"Mom," said Gregory. "Don't you remember last Thursday when we had *Chicken a La Greque Almondine?*"

"Yeah, but..."

Greg plowed on oblivious to my feelings. "Remember how you used that hairy can of salmon instead of the chicken? Then when you didn't have any almonds or almond flavoring, you used peppermint?"

"So, that wasn't one of my more successful attempts, but you'll admit it was unusual!"

"Sure," grimaced Amy. "It tasted like Salmon flavored chewing gum in watery milk sauce."

They were ganging up on me again. You can try and try your best to please your family, but sometimes it's just not enough! They clustered around me like flies around one of my chocolate cakes.

"Mrs. Toon always makes a menu for the whole week, then gets the ingredients." This from Robin who has no sense of adventure.

"Her kids never get the bends on Thursdays!"

I was beginning to feel unappreciated! I tried to stare them down. I asked:

"Do you want to put a bridle on my creative inventiveness?"

"Yes!"

"Yes!"

"Yes!"

That cut me to the quick! I heated up some dried milk and chili powder with the sour sherry.

Carefully, I poached four eggs in it and dumped it all on top of the tired chinese noodles.

Then I scraped it down for the cat, and we went to MacDonalds.

Psst Kid! Ya Want Some Hot Salami?

I used to hate cleaning my refrigerator. Then I hit on the "Combs-Free-Competition-Method." This involves two major principles:

<u>Principle #1:</u> No child ever wants his or her siblings to have one more of anything than he or she has. Even if it is something they loathe and despise, they will cram it down their little gullets to keep it out of friend sibling's hands!

<u>Principle #2:</u> You can slock off ANYTHING at a final clearance sale.

I work it like this:

The day comes when I can't find the balogna unless I first remove:

> a. The pickle jar with one half soggy pickle in it.

    b. The opened coke bottle (which is lying on its side, dribbling its contents into the potato salad).

    c. Three pieces of stale cheese (two wrapped in tired foil, the third nude except for its green, mold coating).

    d. One tennis ball (hidden by Greg so Amy wouldn't find it).

It's "COMBS' FREE COMPETITION DAY!" I wait until the first kid walks into the kitchen (which they do on the average of three per minute).

"PSST! Kid!" I whisper, grabbing Greg by the collar and dragging him over to the partially opened refrigerator door, "Ya want a piece of cheese? Your sister had two!"

"Why can't I have two?" He demands.

I make an incredible show of fighting him off, and then succumb, handing him the two dried out hunks of cheddar.

"Don't tell Robin you had two! I'll let her have this nice moldy one to look at under the microscope."

"Let me! Let me!"

"I don't know…" He grabs it while I pretend to think about it, shoves it in his pocket, then leaps for the door.

Amy comes in.

"How come Greg has two pieces of cheese and a lump in his pocket?"

"I gave them to him so he wouldn't see this nice apple I've been saving for you." I hold my hand over the bad spot on the worn out Red Delicious (quelle misnomer!) and shine it up on my shirt. "It's the last one," I smile tenderly, "and I'm not going to buy apples again for a month!" She whisks it away from me like a fantastic treasure, then slips away into the living room.

Ye old teenager stumbles into the kitchen, her wet hair hanging over her face, one eye balefully peeking out at me. She's known me for a while. She's suspicious.

"What's to eat?"

"You're just in time. I was going to fix a submarine sandwich for your sister, but as long as you're here, you get it!"

Before I can exhale, she's used up the half loaf of stale French bread, the two pieces of curly salami, the soft tomato, three pieces of limp lettuce, the last of the Miracle Whip and topped it off with the lone piece of soggy, dill pickle.

That leaves me with two cans of Yum-Yum cat food and a gray, fuzzy can of Fido Bits.

The dog takes care of the Yum-Yum, and I grab the cat…

"PSST! KITTY!…The dog's not around…"

Please Pass the Watermelon, I've Got a Headache

My husband came home one day to find me lying supine on the couch, a slice of chilled watermelon on my head.

"Mother, Mother! Where are you?" I called softly.

"What's with the watermelon?" My husband questioned.

"It's been one of those days," I answered, "and all the washcloths are Barbie blankets."

"Do you want to tell me about it?" He asked, gently pulling the watermelon seeds out of my hair.

"I guess it all started when I cut my thumb putting the Elmer's Glue on the sandwiches."

"Elmer's glue?"

"Amy broke the glue bottle in her room, but managed to scrape most of it up and put it in a mayonnaise jar. Then she left it out on the counter. I thought the mayonnaise was a little sticky!"

"How did you cut yourself?"

"The knife stuck on a piece of bread, and I rammed my thumb right into it!

He observed my thumb. which was wrapped up in toilet paper, held in place with foil.

"We out of Bandaids?"

"I bought two boxes yesterday, but the only box I could find today had two caterpillars and a dead grasshopper in it."

"That reminds me," he said. "I saw some poor child down the street who must have been in a horrible accident. He was so covered with bandages he could hardly walk."

"That was your son. He fixed all his mosquito bites."

"Who was the poor ragged kid with him? I've never seen such tattered clothes in my life!

"That was your daughter, the tie-dye queen. Her Chlorox bottle got away from her this afternoon. She's going to need all new clothes."

My husband winced. "That'll cost a fortune."

"Maybe not. The new rector called today and saw her. She told him all her clothes looked like that. I think we'll be getting a package of things from the mission barrel any minute."

"Anything else new?"

"Nothing, except there was a very important call for you. I copied down the number and you were supposed to call immediately when you got home."

"Where is it?"

"On the counter, but don't bother!"

"Why not?"

"Greg filled my pen with his disappearing ink, and the message is long gone."

My husband cut himself a piece of watermelon, slapped it on his head and joined me.

177

Jane Hallock Combs

Whacking Out Prejudice

My mother was prejudiced. Her finely tuned prejudice (passed on to me en toto) was not against *people* but against snakes. She killed one once with a rock. I prefer a seven iron.

I try to be sensible. I try to rationalize my feelings ... but snakes slither so! If they only had legs and feet they wouldn't bother me.

Picture a snake, any kind of snake equipped with cute, little legs, and tiny feet scampering though the grass. People would like them ... (mostly). Snakes could develop a whole new persona. Think of lizards. They're reptilian ... but cute. It's the legs. Take the legs away and you've got little, bitty snakes. Not cute. So much for rationalizing. It's a gut thing.

I've tried not to pass my prejudices along to my children. I think I've succeeded. My daughter, Robin, had a pet garter snake, Little Spike. He lived in Robin's room in an old aquarium. He even moved with us when we bought a house in Connecticut ... an old house with lots of nooks and crannies ... nice places for an escaped snake to hide. I had visions. Not good ones.

The visions helped me convince Robin Spike would be happier released in our back yard. Spike sunbathed on our walls for years. He was a lot more relaxed than I was when we'd meet.

If you don't want to pass a prejudice on to the next generation, you must be stern with yourself and learn to hide your gut reactions. If your kids see you jumping up and down, shouting and invoking the diety while beating on a snake with a seven iron, the children are going to: a.) see this as appropriate behavior and follow suit, or, b.) think you are nuts and decide never to visit you in the nursing home.

I tried to keep my cool in front of my children when a snake was anywhere in the vicinity. With Greg it wasn't easy.

When we moved to Florida, Greg was 10. His best friend, Billy, turned out to be a naturalist. I discovered this one day when Greg and I had been invited to Billy's house to meet the family. They were all actively involved with the local "Nature Trail." Nice family.

I sat sipping a glass of iced tea, getting acquainted with Billy's mother when Billy, grinning, ran into the room to show me a special treasure of his. A bucket filled with damp Spanish Moss, brimming with eggs. It wasn't near Easter. *Those* were not Easter eggs.

"Oh, my," I smiled, "What kind of eggs are those, dear (thinking quail? chicadee?)"

"They're Yellow Rat Snake eggs," Billy quivered with enthusiasm as he stuck the bucket of snake eggs under my nose so I could see them better.

"I've got more in the other room. They're going to hatch any time! Wanna see?"

I choked on my tea and declined the opportunity to see his entire collection of snake eggs, envisioning them leaping out of their shells to latch onto me.

"Billy's always been fascinated by snakes," his mom said leaning over to pour me more iced tea. I looked up at her and a movement in the chandelier above the table caught my eye.

"What's that?" I stammered, pointing at the slithering something weaving its way between the light bulbs. At that moment Billy burst back into the room. He reached up into the chandelier and hauled out a three foot long, mean eyed, yellow snake which proceeded to coil itself around his arm.

"This is Emily, my best yellow rat snake. Isn't she cool?" Billy held his arm out toward me so I could better admire said snake. I was beside myself. Myself was not happy.

"You want to hold it?" Billy said in a voice conveying a sense of the great honor being done me. He didn't let just ANYONE hold Emily.

Oh my god! I became accutely aware of Greg, standing beside me, watching my every reaction. I couldn't jump up, scream hysterically and run out the door. I did the only thing I *could* do.

In my bravest moment ever, I stretched out my hand, sucked in my breath, and stammered, "Why not. She looks like a nice snake."

Billy unpeeled Emily from his arm and handed her to me. *I didn't faint!* The snake, a dry, friendly sort wrapped itself around my bare arm then slipped up and around the back of my neck. My hair contracted. "HA! HA! Ha!" I laughed, while my stomach turned pirouettes. *"Isn't this neat?"* I felt my esophogus recoiling into my epiglottus or something. I was a *liar*! But I hardly quivered ... actually I was frozen in place. I couldn't move if I wanted ... and OH how I WANTED.

Emily wound her way slowly down my other arm. When she finally finished the endless trip, I greenly handed her back to the smiling Billy. Greg beamed at me. I was the mother of all cool.

"That certainly is SOME snake!" I tried to start breathing, and then I gulped down the dregs of my iced tea swearing never to set foot in that house again. I didn't! EVER!

My grand plan succeeded though. My kids are grown and not afraid of snakes. They also think I am SO cool. You see, passing prejudice down between generations *can* be destroyed. I have demonstated it.

However, I still have this irrational gut reaction about snakes. I will *never* LIKE them! As soon as it warms up some more, I'll be watching for them. Until they grow cute, little legs, I'll keep my seven iron handy.

Jane Hallock Combs

Resilience

When we lived in Rochester, New York, it irked my friend, Lyn, that anyone north of the Mason-Dixon line should build a swimming pool. I remember one day she said:

"Consider the length of our summers! You peel the cover off, crack the ice, take a dip and pack the pool back up for the winter!"

"You're bitter!" I said.

"No, I'm not!" said Lyn, tearing open a large packing case.

"Just because I have neighbors with a pool set two and a half inches from our property line, who don't speak to me or my kids, doesn't make me bitter." The case open, Lyn started removing little orange boxes and lining them up on the counter.

"If those people want to ignore my perspiring children hanging, panting on the pool fence, that's their business." Lyn was making a second layer of little orange boxes on top of the ones already lined up.

"Just because their dog empties my garbage twice a day and fertilizes my tomato plants is not just cause for me to react bitterly.

"The day that I was sitting outside trying to catch a breath of air, when the thermometer read a hundred and three, and I heard those people invite a stray dog into the pool for a swim, it hardly bothered me. I just packed up my palm fan and my melted down iced-tea and dragged myself back into the house. I didn't make obscene phone calls to them or even kick their dog."

Lyn's pile of orange boxes was growing so high it half obscured her window.

"Help me with this other case," she said, opening the door to the garage where I saw two more grocery cases just like the one she had finished emptying onto the counter.

She pushed and I pulled the heavy case into the kitchen.

"The other night when they had the neighborhood splash party and didn't invite us, I could have become bitter. When I couln't get to sleep at 2:30 because of the noise and their pool light pouring in through our bedroom window, I could have been, but chose NOT to be bitter. One must be resilient! One must be able to bounce back from life's little disappointments and upsets."

She cracked open the second case and started lining up more little orange boxes on the other counter. I looked closer.

"They must have had an awfully good special on clear gelatine at the Market! You have a twelve year supply!"

She turned to me with a satanic twinkle in her eye and chuckled a dark, devious chuckle.

"Tonight," she said, "the temperature is supposed to dip into the thirties, and I am dumping all this gelatine into THAT pool and letting it *gel* solid!"

I was sure if all the neighorhood had Lyn's resilience, her neighbors would just bounce right back!

OUR TOWN...and Welcome to It!

(Note: This tale and the previous one were written when I lived in Rochester, N.Y...they are both a a little bit stretched. Living in Rochester can do that to you.)

Rochester, N.Y. was, in its early days, known for its flour mills. Today it's nicknamed "Flower City" (an interesting name for a place famed for its snow and cold.)

When I lived there, I worked for a real estate agency. Occasionally I plowed through the eternal snow to the airport to welcome new prospects flying in from out of state. It was easy to recognize those who arrived from the deep South.

One day I was picking up some folks from Tennessee. I recognized them the moment I saw the woman clinging hysterically to the plane's stair rail, crying for her mother. I rushed out and helped the husband peel his wife's fingers one by one from the metal railing.

"Welcome to 'Flower City'!" I shouted over her sobbing. She stopped in the middle of a gasp as though someone had clapped a hand across her mouth.

"See Harry! Ah told you it had to be the wrong place!" She ducked under Harry's arm and tried to sprint back up the plane's steps.

The first thing Rochester Real Estate agents are taught is the flying tackle. I brought her down before she'd gotten past the fifth step.

"No, no Mrs. Beauregard. Rochester IS 'Flower City'!

"But look at that snow and this her-ah sky! I want to go home!"

"What's the matter with our sky?" I asked defensively. It was no more gray than usual.

"It's so dreary!"

"Dreary! Honey, this is one of our brighter days! Just look at those pale, gray rain clouds, scudding gaily across the soft opalescence of that bank of high, prevailing snow cumuli. If that isn't

189

cheery, I don't know what is! You should see our DREARY days!"

I got a hammerlock on her just before she could bolt back up the stairway.

"I know you are just going to love it here in the winter fun capital of the North!" I bubbled. "Do you ski much?"

"Ah never have skied." She sniffed. Then brightening perceptably, she admitted, "But ah always did have a hankering to go sledding!"

"Why, that's great!" I said. "As we tell all our winter enthusiasts, 'Rochester boast nine months of winter and only three months of poor sledding'."

I began wondering about that woman. The stewardesses were trying to raise the stairs, but Mrs. Beauregard was now gripping the rails with both hands. I began to think she would be slid like a pancake into the belly of the plane along with the stairs.

After we pulled her loose, Harry and I carted her, toes dragging through the frost on the runway, towards the terminal. Harry tried to shout over his wife's whining. "It must really be beautiful when the sunlight reflects off all that snow."

"Oh it is, it is!" I enthused. "I remember last year on February 22nd at 2:23 P.M. The sun came out for a minute and fifty nine seconds. It was gorgeous!"

"Tell us," said Harry, whose voice seemed to be weakening, probably from the exertion of dragging his wife. "What are some of the other winter sports around here?"

"Well, besides my husband," I chortled, "we've got 'car betting'."

"Car betting?"

"Yeah! Rochesterians bet on whose new car is going to rust out first from the road salt. That's a lot of fun. What kind of a car do you have?"

"A new Ford mini-van."

"Well, if you're a betting man, better figure its good for at least four or five months before the bottom drops out."

"I want to go back to Memphis!" That woman was working herself up again! Harry tightened his grip on her:

"Darlin', now a place that's called 'Flower City' can't be all that bad, can it?"

I didn't tell him.

Interpretation...Say What?

Lots of things are open to interpretation. My bank account for example. Every month, the poor, little man at the bank sits down with me and holds my hand while I blubber a bit, and he interprets the bank statement for me. Then I hold his hand while he blubbers a lot and I try to interpret my check book for him. It's an interesting relationship and one where careful interpretation is vital (particularly should his wife or my husband come into the bank on one of our days when we are striving for a meeting of the minds.)

Interpretation is crucial too when dealing with Homo Sapiens Junior. If you don't watch it, you'll find yourself out on a limb while he's sawing it off.

One day Gregory came to me and asked:

"Mommy, when we finish living here, where do we go?"

"Ah, my love, I'm so glad you asked me that," I lied through tightly clenched teeth.

"When at last we finish shuffling off this mortal coil," I said, "we have several interesting possibilities…" I mentally thumbed through my copy of "Death, the Fun Way to Explain it to Children" and stopped at page sixteen.

"Remember when Flibo, the Goldfish, died?"

"Yeah, and we flushed him down the…"

"That was a poor example … let's take the sparrow who passed away on the patio last week."

"The one that bashed his stupid head on the picture window?" Greg was sweet, but had never been known for his sensitivity.

"Yes, dear." I said. "Remember how we wrapped him in tissue paper and put him in a dear little shoe box then we dug a hole in the ground and buried him?"

194

"Yeah, but..."

"Well, he's resting from a long and a happy life now."

"No, he's not. The cat dug him up last week."

"Dear, I said, shoving the subject into a slight shift ..." when we 'leave' here, our bodies may be buried, but our souls waft happily up to heaven."

"Can Jimmy come too?"

"Not unless its his 'wafting' time also." Things didn't seem to be going very well.

"But, I mean, where are we all going when we stop living here?" He's a bit dense sometimes. I tried again.

"Our old, tired, used-up bodies can either go to 'Hillcrest Happy Havens' while our spirits flit forever onward and upward through endless infinity ... then, of course, there's cremation, but that's another matter..."

"Well, I was just wondering." Greg looked at me with his small brow wrinkling." Jimmy asked me where we were going when we left here, and I told him 'back to Kentucky…'"

It's all a question of interpretation. Think I'll go balance my check book

Cowboys and Other Foreign Students

Teaching English to foreign students is an exhilarating experience. Their names and the pronunciation of the same is another matter. At one time I had in my class a husband and wife whose first names were Paysineth and Sampasanya. Their last names I never attempted.

When I think of memorable names though, I think of the first great wave of Vietnamese refugees to come into this country. Ninety-seven percent of them had as a last name "Nguyen". Pronounced "Negoóyen" maybe? No!" NWynn" was the correct pronunciation.

Vietnamese *first* names were not too difficult and some times provided a little break in the day's monotony. At one point I had in my class two gentlemen named "HA", one named "Hi", another named "Hee", a fifth named "Ho", and yet another named "Who." If ever things got too dull, or I was in serious need of a chuckle, all I would have to say was:

"Ha, Ha, Hi, Hee, Ho and Who, would you mind going to the board for a minute? We're going to work on" whatever it was we needed to work on at that moment.

The names were fun, but tricky to keep straight particularly since so many of them had the same last name. One of my supervisors (who was sorely in need of retirement) never could understand why I had so many "Nguyens" in my class. He thought I was padding the roll.

"Just think of it as the Vietnamese equivalent of Smith or Jones" I told him. The last thing we needed to do was worry about NAMES!" At that point we had 160 students of all levels with four teachers and two aides of dubious expertise trying to cope.

I had frequent dreams involving boat-loads of refugees pulling up to the door of our class to unload eighty or ninety non-English speakers right into the crowded class room. I would have to crawl across students to get to my desk. There were times when reality seemed close to the nightmare

But the students names provided moments of lightness. HA, HA, HI, HEE, HO and WHO, the chuckling board group, was fun. Then there were "The Cowboys".

One busy day, we had eight brothers come in to class together. Their last name was spelled CAO, pronounced "Cow". I don't remember all their first names. We tended to refer to them in a group as "The Cowboys." What else?

For the most part, The Cowboys' English was not too bad. And they were very bright. They ranged in age from 19 to 26. A joy to have in class.

When they told us their younger brother, who had just arrived in St. Petersburg, would be starting school the following week, the teachers were all pleased.

"He does not speak any English," they informed us.

"No problem", we thought. With all his older brothers to help him, little brother would pick up English in no time.

The problem we had not anticipated was the name thing. While his brothers had nice sensible first names like "Han", "Tran" or "Van", baby Cowboy had a name that gave us a bit of a pause.

With the help of his brothers, the sunny seventeen year old filled out his enrollment sheet, then brought it to me. I looked at the name. Yes … the Cowboy bunch was expanding! We knew that. I studied the enrollment form. Last name CAO. First name …"PHUC".

Oh my! My Vietnamese pronunciation was not the best, but I could take a rough guess at baby brother's name. To be sure, I asked an older brother how to pronounce it. He pronounced it. Yeah! It was pronounced as it was spelt.

I took the big brothers aside.

"We've got a problem. Your brother's name is not a good name in English." I made a wry face, "In fact, it's pretty bad."

I had a mental image of the reactions of Americans to the name "P-H-U-C"... particularly linked up with the last name "Cow".

"But is a good name in Vietnamese ... very common." Said the big brothers.

"Does he have a nickname, or ANY other name we could use?" I was clutching at straws.

"No. No nickname. Just his name. Is good name!"

I could see I was getting close to insulting them.

"Does his name have a meaning in Vietnamese?" I asked.

"Yes, it means good luck."

That was it...

"OK! How about calling him "Lucky! That would be a good American nickname for your brother."

And that's what his name became. *Lucky Cow* was an attention getting name, but not as attention getting as his real one would have been!

Warm Fuzzies Anyone? (Please!)

Christmas is a warm, fuzzy time. I know. I'm partially responsible. I knit warm fuzzies. My family begs me not to, but I persist.

Something about the cool days of Fall makes me twitch with desire for the feel of warm wool slipping through my fingers and the click-click of flashing needles. I am a fast, good knitter. I can cable, twist, yarn-over, seed and popcorn with THE BEST. I knit beautiful stuff.

If only it ever fit … anyone!.

I found I had a problem when I was in college. I made an argyle sock for my boyfriend back home. I never gave it to him. I hate ridicule.

It was a beautiful sock, but unfortunately singular … a LARGE, singular, argyle sock. He could have easily put both feet (and a small golf bag) into that sock. But what lovely knitting! The colors blended and twisted just right. If it hadn't been so huge, and had had a mate, it would have been perfect!

Fortunately the boyfriend and I broke up before the question of "Where the heck are those argyles!" ever arose. At least I didn't have to have memories of hysterical laughter following me down through the years. At least not from him.

Of course there was the ski sweater I made my brother. It would have looked nice on Dave, if he'd been able to get it on over his head.

I can see him now, standing by the Christmas tree with the top of his head peeking out from the sweater neck while the sleeves (a teensy bit long) dangled down from his finger tips almost to his knees. Perhaps it wasn't one of my best efforts, but it hardly merits hysterical laughter ... *after twenty five years!* Come on!

So I've had problems! Like the beautiful, lacy sweater I made myself that matched the skirt made from material purchased at the same time.

Well…it would have matched the skirt if the skirt hadn't worn out before I finished the sweater.

The sweater was made on size "0" needles with yarn as thin as spider web. When I finished it, it looked magnificent draped casually over my shoulders. It's good it did because I couldn't force my arms into its "tailored sleeves with knit-in cuffs and hems". If I *had* been able to shove my arms into the sleeves, it wouldn't have helped much. They measured 2 1/2 times the length of my arms! Oh well! It was gorgeous anyway.

Then there was Bill's trauma. The first year we were married, I knitted him an incredibly beautiful, Irish Fisherman's sweater … off-white, covered with twisty cables, intricate stitches, and little pop corn bubbles. I had to check the pattern before each stitch because it constantly changed. No two rows or stitches were alike.

"I don't think it's going to be big enough!" This from Big Bill.

"No problem!" I would calm him. "It'll be big enough."

"Looks small to me!" He'd groan, yanking at a popcorn stitch. "What's this big lump you've got here?"

"It's a popcorn stitch! Leave it alone! And don't worry about the sweater! Patterned stuff always scrunches up when you knit. It only LOOKS small. It'll be bigger when I block it!"

I was right. When I washed and blocked it, I could easily have slip covered our huge recliner with it ... or possibly the love seat. Small it was not!

Luckily, a book salesman stopped by our house en route to Nebraska. A big book man who stood about 6'7" and weighed in at least 350 lbs! The sweater fit him perfectly; to the best of my knowledge, it is still keeping this large stranger warm somewhere in the depths of Nebraska.

For a while I gave up knitting for adults and spent my time and yarn whipping up woolies for the children in the family … of whom there were plenty! If something didn't fit one, it was sure to fit another. Of course, sometimes their mothers would have to push their little heads through the neck holes, but children are malleable, and tight necks keep out drafts.

As the kids got older, though, they allowed as to how they'd prefer a nice new toothbrush for Christmas instead, or they'd ask me if I would donate the current sweater to some poor, needy child in their names.

I can take a hint.

This year our church prepared layettes for new born babies. We gave the layettes to the hospital. At last I'd found my mission. I could use up some of the yarn left over from a couple of disastrous baby sweaters I'd been working on. (If ever one of my friends gives birth to a short, 20 pound baby with long arms I'm already prepared with several sweaters.) With the leftover yarn, surely I could manage booties that would fit newborns.

You wouldn't think booties could get away from you, but they can! I followed the pattern exactly, but they ended up looking like pastel, golf club-head covers.

I don't know… sometimes I feel like forgetting about knitting, but it's cold out today, and the fire is roaring. Maybe Bill would like a complete set of matching pastel, golf, club-head covers for Christmas!

On Judging Book Covers

You know the old "saw" about not judging a book by its cover? True (unless it shows a lovely lady in decolletage being pawed by a handsome devil with flowing hair ... take it from me ... that one's a "Romance Novel" for sure!)

But in the real world what you see is not always what you get. Especially when you're teaching foreign students. I learned that quickly back in the 80's when I had a huge class filled with people of all descriptions from every part of the world. The plump, little, Vietnamese gentleman who worked as an orderly in one of the hospitals had been a doctor in Vietnam and would be again if he ever mastered English and could be certified.

Paco, the Mexican who walked into our class all dressed in black leather with chains dangling from his waist and a surly look on his face.

TROUBLE! I thought. Yet Paco turned out to be a sweet, gentle person. He had never been to school a day in his life, but was one of the best and brightest students I've ever known.

Then there was Fiesel whom I REALLY pegged wrong.

I'm not sure when Fiesel showed up in class. You hardly ever knew he WAS there. At some point I was aware that there was this really mousey looking middle aged man tucked away somewhere in the back of the room whose voice was softer than a mole's skin.

A lot of our work was on pronunciation, sentence completion and conversation. Fiesel's soft voice was a handicap.

"What was that, Fiesel?"

"Could you say that again, Fiesel" That seemed to be a lot of my side of our mutual conversations. This man was painfully shy and didn't mingle much with the other students.

What taumas he must have had in his life to make him so timid and wary I thought.

One day the class was sitting in a circle, completing sentences which I would begin for them. It was always next to impossible to hear Fiesel's answers. He sat in his grey sweat suit in a far corner of the circle. (You didn't know circles could have corners? Well Fiesel could always find one. His chair was always edged back a bit). Anyway, the sentence the students were completing for me was, "One thing I REALLY love to do is…" I'd gotten the normal completions like "swim," "walk on the beach," "play with my baby," and then we got to Fiesel.

"Fiesel, what is one thing that you really LOVE to do?"

The quiet voice whispered something.

"Could you speak up, Fiesel?"

He raised his voice a teensy bit.

"One thing I really love to do is jump out of airplanes."

I thought my hearing had gone bad. "Jump out of airplanes?" I asked.

"Yes," he whispered.

"Do you jump out of airplanes often?" I questioned.

"Not too much now. My wife doesn't like it."

I couldn't let this go. "How did you ever get started doing that?"

In a very quiet voice he said,

"I had to do it for my work."

What kind of work would have a plumb, mousey man jumping out of planes?

I asked him (leaving out the part about him being plump and mousey.)

"For fifteen years I worked for INTERPOL." I couldn't picutre our quiet, little Fiesel working for the daring International Police force! "Many times I had to jump out of planes at night into foreign countries. It was very exciting. But very dangerous."

I bet!

"Now I just jump out of planes for fun and for exhibitions. Eet ees easy to land in a painted circle on the ground when eet ess daytime! What ess hard is to land on some rough place you don't know about in the middle of thee night. "He got a small, mischieveous grin on his gray face, "But eet was *WONDERFUL!*"

We had a real live JAMES BOND in our class, but you would certainly never know it. I tried on a number of occasions to get him to tell us some of the adventures he had had, but that was all hush hush and so was he. The only time he told us anything was when I had the students give five minute talks on their favorite recreation.

During the question/answer section after Fiesel's talk on parachuting, someone asked him if he hadn't been afraid the first time he had jumped from a plane. Then our James Bond let us in on the only international secret we'd ever get from him:

"I tell you, I was so scared, I pee in my pants!"

Jane Hallock Combs

I Seldom Need Supervision

My first full time teaching assignment, in Florida, was to NEED, a facility for adult mentally handicapped persons. There were several classrooms and a large sheltered workshop. A fine, well-known facility filled with people as varied as any cross section of the population. Some of my students I loved. Some I didn't.

It was a light teaching assignment with six fifty minutes classes of ten students per class. The instruction was not strenuous. Some students would fall asleep due to their medications. Others would be working on their individual prescriptions: how to count to ten (or three) or to make change for a quarter. It wasn't intellectually stimulating, but it had its interesting moments.

When not in my classroom, students worked in the sheltered workshop next door. You walked through the workshop to get to the coffee machine or rest rooms.

I remember the day I approached the restroom and heard great crashing noises coming from within. As I opened the door, a very large woman with wild, red hair came flying towards me waving a lethal looking broom beating on everything in her path. I ducked just in time and watched as she careened off into the workshop to be stopped in mid flight by several observant caseworkers.

"What happened," I asked someone at the coffee machine.

"Oh, Emma saw a spider in the rest room. She got excited." SHE got excited! My blood pressure was doing a Fandango. The poor spider probably committed suicide in the commode.

I learned to walk carefully through the workshop after that. You never knew what would happen. One day, heading toward my classroom,

I spotted a man striding towards me, his hand outstretched.

"Hi, I'm Tom," he said grinning.

We shook hands. Tom had a firm grip … a *very* firm grip. Tom didn't release my hand. We stood shaking hands for 3 1/2 minutes as Tom repeatedly introduced himself to me. Then he spotted my fingers and continued to hold my hand captive while he fondled my fingers and stroked my fingernails. It looked like I might be there for good.

"He's not dangerous" a case worker assured me as he disconnected Tom from my hand.

" He just likes hands … and FEET! Try not to wear sandals in here!," he said. "I mean Tom REALLY LIKES FEET!"

My eyes followed Tom as he ambled back to his work station, his hand stuck out again in case he met any other unsuspecting person. Three caseworkers and two clients side-stepped Tom as he came in their direction.

It was strange working at NEED, but never DULL! And it had one nice advantage. We county teachers and our aides were left pretty much on our own.

Our "Principal" at the adult center downtown collected our reports and gave us our pay checks, but other than that stayed as far from us as he possibly could. I think I was there for at least six months before I ever saw a trace of our "Supervisor."

The day she was due to visit, our teaching team had gotten our room looking schoolish. We'd roused our sleepier students into some kind of action. We were doing creative exercises of making change to ten cents. We had a "Welcome, Ms. Wexford" sign taped to the door.

Ms. Wexford didn't show up at the appointed hour. Then it was time for the class to change.

As the students (who'd missed their regular nap times) filed out and the next group stumbled in, I dashed out the door to see if I could spot our missing supervisor.

Around the corner of the building was a walk leading to the parking lot. Half way between the parking lot and our building, I saw her.

Frozen in place in the middle of the sidewalk with a wild, panicked look on her face, Ms Wexford stood with foot-fetish Tom stretched out on the lawn beside her holding on to her foot (she'd worn sandals. I 'd forgotten to tell her).

Tom held her foot with one hand while stroking her toes with the other.

She'd worn Blazing Red nail polish. Tom's most favorite kind. Tom had a blissful look on his face. My supervisor's face was beyond description. I think she was crying. I know she was blubbering.

It's not a pretty sight to see an Adult Education Supervisor falling apart at the seams, but when I rescued her, I became her favorite teacher for life. I always got very good assignments after that ... and I sure didn't have to worry about any more supervision ... at least not at NEED!

Jane Hallock Combs

Part 3

"Shakespeare, Dogs, and Filthy Beasts"

Writing Vs. Art

Do artists ever get artist's block? If they do, I've never heard about it. Painting's got to be easier than writing.

Artists just sit down, stick a brush in a pot of color and start splashing around. Lots of fun! If you sketch, you can just sketch away drawing any old thing. Then you sell your creation. Piece of cake!

I took up drawing for a while.

During a dull winter, when writer's block held me in its grip like a tick on the Lab's nose, I picked up the book "Drawing on the Right Side of the Brain". It's supposed to stimulate the creativity lurking somewhere in everyone. The author insists ANYONE can draw!

The book has all kinds of exercises in it designed to bring out the potential artist in one. Some of the exercises involve drawing things. I was encouraged to draw strange things: pine cones, crumpled up pieces of paper (something of which a writer always has lots), and an up-side-down copy of a sketch by Rembrandt. If you aim for success, aim high I always say, but why an "up-side-down" picture of Rembrandt to copy? Did Rembrandt frequently draw up-side-down? Je ne sais pas.

I always like to fling a little French around when I'm in a writer's block ... (it makes me feel couth even if I'm not sure what the words mean! I strive for couth!)

Anyway, while staring at the object you plan to draw (moldy pine cone, crumpled up piece of paper or up-side-down Rembrandt) intently, you try to draw it on paper WITHOUT looking at the paper!

Now come-on! Surely even Rembrandt occasionally looked at his canvases ... even if he did draw up-side-down.

After six months of scattered sketching, I had a notebook full of weird drawings. My favorite is the view of my bare left foot seen from the vantage point of my cellulite surrounded knee. It's not bad if you're into feet, knees, and cellulite, but I don't think I'll hang it in the living room.

That leads me to the thought of the advantages that artists have over writers. I have several artist friends. I don't always talk about it, but it's fun to walk into their homes and look at the new works of art hanging on their walls. People can walk around and "ooh" and "aah" over the latest master ... or mistress piece. If they don't care for the art especially, they can at least "ooh" and "aah" over the frames! But writers can't hang their stuff up on the walls. Well maybe a cover or two ... but who wants to look at a book cover stapled to the wall? And the book itself? It's hard to grab friends by the neck and say, "Here's a nice little thing I'd like you to read. It's only

180,000 words ... shouldn't take you long." Lose more friends that way.

If an artist has a block they can always dump the cat in some paint and drag it around on the canvas. They then sell it as art nouveau or something or other. The cat doesn't like it a lot, but it's a technique.

A writer "in block" sharpens a lot of pencils, kicks the computer, and throws French phrases around ... Anything to delay getting down to the writing itself.

Well, "Merci beau coup" and "Il-n-a-pas de quoi". The block is hanging around my neck, like ... what's the word?? ..."a BLOCK"! Which is probably why they call it that. Right now, I've got a deadline to meet. I've got to go scribble ... or maybe I'll do a picture of my *right* foot as seen from the vantage point of my celulite-coated knee. Then I'd have a matched set of pictures ... suitable for framing. Why should artists have ALL the fun?

The Importance of Practice

Practice makes perfect. It pays off ... in the animal world as well as the human. I practiced my piano scales for forever. It never made me a musician, but I can crank out a scale at the drop of a hat.

When I lived in Florida, our next door neighbors owned a dog whose proper name I've forgotten. We always called him "Little Yip." A beautiful looking white Maltese with little discernible intelligence, "Little Yip" continually practiced his ear-piercing, nasty noise that substituted for a bark.

After eight years of living next door to us, "Little Yip" still didn't recognize my husband or me as anyone he had ever seen before.

When I worked in my office which backed up on Little Yip's property, he would stand by the fence yipping until I would finish whatever it was

I was trying to do. Let us attempt some yard work, and "Little Yip" would alert the entire neighborhood that there were dangerous folk afoot. BEWARE! BEWARE!

Speaking of dangerous, the yipper one day made the mistake of yipping at Beau, the HUGE, powerful Rottweiller who lived on the back side of Little Yip's property.

For all his size and power, Beau lived a sedate, rather boring life in his small, fenced-in yard. His owners, both working, couldn't give him all the exercise he needed. Nevertheless, Beau was a laid-back sort of dog … never a problem to the neighbors or anyone. A nice dog.

Beau usually ignored small nuisances like "You-Know-Who." I was out in our yard, pruning roses the day Beau gave Yip his come-up-ance. Yip hadn't noticed I was out there. Normally, he would have rushed the fence on his tiny, fluffy legs, yipping his heart out at the perceived danger of a big, blond woman with rose clippers in her hands who might at any moment burst through the chain-linked fence separating us to do bodily harm to him and his (a thought that became increasingly appealing to me). But Yip hadn't spotted me because he was intent on Beau, the aging, phlegmatic Rottweiller.

As Beau stared at the corner of the fence, the berserk little dog was leaping up and down in a frenzy of high decibel yipping attempting to save the world once and for all from dear Beau. I watched thinking, if Beau were any other big dog he would have torn the fence down and eaten little Yip. But violence wasn't in Beau. He tolerated the nasty performance and ear splitting clamor with dignity and poise until he could stand it no longer.

With world weary eyes that spoke volumes, Beau stared intently at the leaping bundle of noise, then calmly lifted his fence-side leg and squirted Yip right in the face. As Yip ... silenced for once … ran back to the haven of his house, Beau, I swear, smiled and ambled home.

Later, I saw Beau's owner in the yard and told her what had happened.

"He got Yip right in the face," I chuckled.

"Yes, Beau could do that!" She said.

"But to be so accurate! Yip was leaping up and down!" I smiled. "That took a lot of skill."

"Yes," my neighbor said. "But Beau gets a lot of practice." She pointed at Beau who was staring intently at a palm tree near their patio. "He gets kind of bored in this little yard so he's got himself a hobby. He has to have something to do."

I noticed Beau lifting his leg at the palm tree.

"All male dogs do that," I said.

"Yeah," she answered, "But do all male dogs squirt LIZARDS off trees?" She laughed. "Beau does. He does it all the time! It gives him something to do! It keeps him entertained. He's had lots of practice!"

Little Yip never bothered Beau again after that. As I said earlier, practice pays off ... for people ... and animals. Excuse me while I go work on my scales.

Good Graciousness!

When granddaughter, Kristie, turned five, she knew all there was to know. My friend, Fran, at whose house we'd been visiting one day, patted Kristie's head and said,

"My, Kristie, you certainly are a smart, little girl."

Kristie cocked an eye at Fran and agreed.

"Yes, I know just about EVERYTHING!" And that was BEFORE she started Kindergarten! Now that she is a college Freshman, she truly knows all that could possibly be known ... but there WAS a time!...

Kristie didn't speak until she was almost three. We used to worry about her ... when we had time to worry! She kept the whole family busy with her non-verbal communications.

Kristie had a wide range of imperious gestures, facial expressions and a huge variety of unmistakable sounds of: pleasure, command, irritation and one that I'm sure meant, "Chop the head off that idiot who is pretending he doesn't know what I mean!"

In the movie "Nell", Nell had her own language ... Kristie had her own sounds and gestures.

"Humpf!" plus a screwed up face and a skinny finger aimed at the cookie jar meant, "Someone hop to it and get me a cookie, quick, or there'll be Hell to pay!"

A tapping of the small foot, combined with pointing at her mouth meant "What ever it is you have, I want it double and RIGHT NOW!"

We all figured she had been an empress, at least, in a previous existence, and, of course, we'd all been her humble servants ... Ha! Make that SLAVES! And so it went. We wondered what would happen when she went to school? Would we have to go along to serve and translate for her at her every beck and call? A distinct possibility!

It was a worry. But at three Kristie suddenly started speaking ... in full blown, grammatically correct sentences. As Grandpa Bill said, she didn't have anything worth talking about until then. When she did, she found her vocal cords ... and fast!

Then, there was no shutting her up. On and on she rattled about the fly on the wall, the fuzz on the floor, the potato on the plate ... anything, everything as long as it kept her mouth moving.

While she prattled on and on, she was also always in motion ... climbing, swinging between the arms of chairs ... turning cartwheels, standing on her head ... An object in motion who never *thought* of resting. Being around her for more than two and a half minutes was exhausting!. I lost weight watching her.

At age five, Kristie started school. The first time her mother, Amy, went in for a parent teacher conference, Amy was nervous.

Jane Hallock Combs

"I hope Kristie doesn't distract the class with all her talking and acrobatics."

The teacher looked at her folder to see if they were talking about the same child.

"No, Kristie is always extremely quiet and well behaved. She just seems to sit and listen. A lovely child. But so quiet! We've been trying to draw her out."

Kristie was a totally different child at school than she was at home.

I learned first hand about her double personality one day. She had called and asked if I would take her with me to my church on Sunday.

"Of course," I said, but began regretting it as soon as we started driving down the palm lined street towards St. Anne of Grace Episcopal. Kristie had not stopped talking since she had gotten into the car. Her mouth flapped in unison with her bouncing around the front seat, trying to see if she could stand on her head in the

234

passenger side and touch the roof of the Mazda with her patent leathers.

A word of caution was obviously in order:

"Kristie," I said, "you know, in church we need to try to sit still and listen. We don't talk except when we're praying ... and we don't jump around a whole lot."

Suddenly, Kristie peeled herself off the car ceiling plopping down bolt upright beside me heaving an enormous, long suffering sigh while rolling her brown eyes around like marbles.

"Mághe!" She chastened me. "I GO TO KINDERGARTEN!" Then she capped this manifesto with the statement: "I am always *gracious* in Kindergarten! I can be *gracious* in church too!"

...And she was! The wooden angel in the sacristy never was as still as Kristie in church. Hands folded in her lap, "Miss Whirling Dervish" was the soul of decorum. I was quiet too. I think I was in shock.

Kristie is almost 18 now. She has her own car. She has a boyfriend. She has a life plan. She intends to be an engineer. She still gets imperious gleams in her dark eyes now and then, and she has a tone of voice that can command attention from all but the dead, but I don't foresee any real problem. I know in time of need, this kid knows how to be gracious!

Grandparenting Made Simple

Lately, I've been tutoring a friend who is an incipient grandparent. I'm helping her learn the finer points of grand parenting.

"What do you think I should have the baby call me?" She asks in her pre-grandparent innocence.

"It's not a problem," I answer.

"I suppose I could be "Mam-maw" like we used to call our grandmother."

"It's not a problem," I reiterate.

"Or Grandmamá!" She brightened.

"Forget it!" I said.

"You don't like Grandmamá?" Pending grandparents are so naive.

"It's not that," I broke the news to her, "You don't really have much say about it. Grandkids will call you whatever they WANT to for reasons known only to God and them." She looked crushed. I think she had really gotten into the "Grandmamá" thing. HA!

I went on:

"The important BIT to remember is that they are going to adore you no matter *what* they call you … *if you work it right!*"

"By the way," she asked, "why do your grand kids call you "Mághe?"

"Well, Tyson had a little syllable reversal problem when he started talking. He tried calling me "Gam ma", but it came out backwards as "Magah"… and Magah…or Mághe "stuck. (I added the accent when the kids learned to write. They thought it was cool.)

"I like that." My friend said. "Mághe sounds exotic, foreign … maybe I'll try it."

"As I said before, it doesn't work like that!

"Robin's kids call me Grandma Go-Go", I went on, "not because I was a dancer in my youth," I said, nipping her next question in the bud, "but because I used to take them places all the time. Whenever they saw me, it was 'Hop in the car and away we go' … hence Grandma Go-go".

I used to get strange looks from people when Robin's kids called me that in public, and one day I suggested to them that Mághe was a nice name and already in use by their cousins, so they could call me that too if they wanted. They thought for a second then said:

"No, we call you *Grandma Go-go*."

It's not the greatest name, but at least it's beats what Amy's kids call their paternal grandfather.

For obscure reasons, Tyson and Kristie named Grandpa Bill Baker, "Grandpa Beeper-Bopper."

"You'll just have to wait" I counseled my friend, "and see what your grand baby calls you. But I promise, it's not likely to be Grandmamá." My friend was starting to look downcast again. I had to brighten her up.

"But remember, whatever they decide to call you, they will absolutely adore you if you follow a few basic rules.

"Which are?…" she quizzed.

"#1. Make cookies and hot chocolate frequently

#2. Love them *UNCONDITIONALLY* and

#3. *Never deny them any wish, no matter how bizarre or out of line it may seem!"*

"But doesn't that lead to problems? You HAVE to deny CHILDREN SOME THINGS!"

She was thinking like a mother! I was going to have to do a complete brainwash on this woman.

"Grandmothers do *NOT HAVE PROBLEMS* with grandchildren. *ONLY FUN!* Grandmas approach things differently. That's how we climb up to the lofty pedestal from which we can be eternally adored by said grandchildren. Listen! You must learn the basic Grandparenting technique!"

I sat her down.

"Let's say you're watching the grand kids and little 'Luly', or whoever, decides it would be fun to paint the walls in her room with hot chocolate pudding so that when she is hungry she can just lick a little off the walls.

"'What a *MARVELOUS* idea!,'" you say, falling immediately in with the child's plans. But then you quickly assume a crestfallen attitude and break the sad news to the child that although YOU think pudding painting is a fantastic and *original* idea, and *you* would go along with it in a minute, the terrible truth is that said child's parents would probably not like it. (Parents are such KILL JOYS!). You then help the child do a little plain, old, finger painting while heaving deep sighs over the lost pudding opportunities..." Trouble is averted, but you are NEVER the heavy.

My friend was a good mother. She's going to have some trouble making the switch to grand parenting ... but I'll be there. I'll help. She'll be fine.

Cousin Phil's Dog

When Cousin Phil was president of a Midwestern College, he and his family lived in a huge, mansion in the middle of a rambling park filled with ancient, towering trees and gentle walk ways.

Phil, at heart always a bit theatrical, felt the only thing lacking in the composition of this picture was the image of the President himself, dressed in leather elbowed tweeds, smoking a Meerschaum, strolling through the quiet park accompanied by an large, elegant dog. Phil had the tweeds and pipe, but no dog!

The thought being father to the deed, Phil, rushed out and bought a great Dane Puppy. "Swifty", at four months already towering over most dogs, seemed perfect for the part. Phil and wife, Anne, were not really dog people and hadn't much of a notion about what they'd gotten into.

Great Danes are nice dogs, but they are not always the brightest, and can have little unforseen problems.

Like the farting. It did seem to be an obsession with Swifty. Not a problem when walking in the park, but in the house was another matter.

"That dog's GOT to go!" Anne would mutter.

A college president often has to host large parties for alumni and faculty. A gigantic dog with odorsome habits could be a detriment.

Before any gala occasion, Phil and Anne would try to sequester Swifty in an upstairs room where he could play with his dog toys and in general circumflatulate to his heart's content.

One year, twenty minutes before the big Christmas party, Phil and Anne, who had not yet isolated Swifty, heard a huge crash come from the living room. Swifty, intrigued by the lights and decorations, had raced across the room hurling himself at the tree knocking it and the decorations flat. With only 20 minutes to go before the guests arrived, Phil and Anne rushed in to see Swifty, a silly smile on his face lying happily atop the flattened Christmas tree amid a mess of wires and broken ornaments. A gauzy angel rested at an angle on top of Swifty's head, the halo circling his eye like a monocle.

Getting the mess straightened out in time was not fun. Let's not think of that.

By the time Swifty was fully grown, his little personal problem had become a major source of concern.

"That dog's got to go!" Anne muttered.

Windows in the house were always flung wide except in times of extreme cold. When visitors came, Swifty was not ony remanded to his room, but was held there by a long chain to insure his seclusion. A friendly, grinning great dane with a little personal problem is not something you want hanging around fragile, elderly Alums from whom one is trying to obtain college bequests.

One day, with Swifty supposedly safe in his room, Phil and Anne were serving tea to an ancient lady who had indicated she would like to leave a large amount to the college. Phil had just about gotten down to the point of her signing on the dotted line when they heard the sickening sounds of large dog clumping down the winding staircase dragging behind him his huge chain. Calump, calump, calump, cachunk, cachunk, cachunk! Unmistakeable.

Phil gave the high sign to Anne who slipped away trying to prevent disaster.

As he continued speaking with the elderly lady, Phil could hear the distinct sounds of wrestling going on on the stairway.

The old alumnus, who was fortunately a little hard of hearing, finally signed the agreement and rose to leave. Phil escorted her to the door as she said:

"These old houses certainly are drafty, and with all the creaky and settling noises around here, I don't know how you ever manage to sleep!"

Phil closed the front door after her departure, then heard a loud crash from the gracious curving stairway and a cry:

"Phil...!"

Anne hadn't broken her leg. Just her dignity.

Maybe it made for a nice image seeing the President of the college dressed in tweeds, smoking a pipe, walking his beautiful dog, but the vision of the President's wife sprawling on the staircase tangled up with a great dane complete with ten foot of chain was not.

I believe after that Swifty left swiftly.

A Concert for Two

Kentucky is bird watching heaven! Coming from Florida (which specializes mostly in seagulls, pelicans and other seabirds) I'm delighted to live on a branch of the "Mississippi Flyway" where the variety of songbirds is seemingly endless.

I had been disappointed in the birds in Florida. The migratory birds seem to pass through cement-coated Pinellas County on their way to greener pastures. They don't sing much in passing, and Robins in Florida (with their fondness for the fermented juice of the Florida Holly berry) seldom sober up long enough to emit even the saddest of sodden sounds.

The only birds who provide consistant song and acrobatics in Florida are the mockingbirds.

We particularly liked the love dances where the male mockingbird would find the highest pinnacle possible, then fling himself upward in a huge, neckbreaking arc before twirling himself back to his original vantage point where he'd sit dizzily hoping that some nubile female friend had noticed his act. If not, he'd do it all again... Probably scrambling his brains worse than glue sniffing.

I don't know about the female mockingbirds, but I know Bill and I were fascinated. We watched one particular mockingbird all that last Florida spring ... a young bachelor who constantly hurled himself skyward from the very top of our neighbors' oak tree providing us with live entertainment while we sipped our coffee or iced tea on the back deck. We laughed over him, rooted for him, and were happy when his antics finally paid off. Through our binoculars we saw not one but two females join him. There was a little arguing, but it all worked out. Ah love!

We had enjoyed the mockingbirds and left bird goodies out for the mockingbird all summer.

Great fun! But our last mockingbird experience was our very best.

When the time came for us to leave Florida for Kentucky, we became engrossed in our packing and all the moving preparations. Who had time to bird watch?

One of our last days there … a heavy, hot, humid afternoon, we decided to take a break and go to the beach.

We picked up beer and chips at one of our favorite beach stands and plopped down on a bench at the edge of Indian Rocks Beach.

We had parked the car in a sandy lot surrounded by Palmento Palms

One palmetto was about two feet in front of the bench we'd sat on. The Palm fronds shaded us from the hot afternoon sun.

While we sat talking about the move to Kentucky and watching the gulls swoop low over the shining water, we became aware that a mockingbird, somewhere in the near vicinity, was practicing his repertoire.

For a minute he'd work on his trills. Then he'd flit to another tree and launch into his immitation of someone whistling for their dog. Then there'd be a brief silence and ... was that a bit of Beethoven coming from still another palmetto? Just a a snatch?

More silence ... then he'd work on his arpheggio's.

Bill and I couldn't spot the great immitator as he moved from tree to tree ... checking out accoustics, I think ... but we could certainly hear him.

Then there was a long silence. During that time, I was overwhelmed with sadness at the thought of leaving Florida, family and friends.

Would Kentucky be kind to a stranger?

Surely there'd be mockingbirds in Kentucky. They'd been a comfort in Florida ... Would they comfort me in Calloway County, Kentucky too?

As I mused, suddenly … right before our eyes, the mockingbird who'd been flitting from tree to tree practicing his best stuff … suddenly was THERE right in front of us in the palmetto shading our bench. He stood on a palm frond on a level with our eyes not two feet away. We didn't dare move. We could have reached out and touched him if we'd wanted.

He looked right at us, and sensing he had a captive and appreciative audience, I swear, he fluffed his feathers, looked us square in the eyes and started in on a very private concert for two. He warbled, he trilled, he segued his dog call between a snatch of Beethoven and an aria that sounded like a thrush in full voice.

The concert went on for three or four minutes while Bill and I sat entranced scarcely daring to breath.

As quickly as it had begun, it was over. The bird paused, dipped his head appropriately, then flew off while Bill and I sat clapping and laughing. A lovely farewell from Florida ... and from a very special friend.

Them Kentucky Cats!

When I first married Bill, I discovered that whenever two or more Kentuckians get together, even if they're total strangers, the very first words out of their mouths always are:

"How 'bout them cats!"

Cat lovers all. That's wonderful! I've always been a feline fancier myself. So, when Bill said we were moving to Kentucky, I figured I'd be in cat heaven. How lovely for Lisbeth, the Persian, and me ... not to mention Big Bill who is Kentuckian down to his boots.

I forgot that Lisbeth, like myself, a New Yorker, had spent her formative years with my mother, at that time an elderly lady who had not expected a whole lot of "work" from Lisbeth per se. Lisbeth was coddled and spoiled. Her only physical exercise involved lying around in wait for a door to open so that she could DASH outside where she would lead Mama on a merry chase avoiding any and all pleas of "Here kitty, kitty. Nice kitty!"

Lisbeth got a little exercise. My mama got a lot. Mama's exercise varied between chasing Lisbeth all over the great outdoors and rolling Lisbeth's food for the cat indoors.

"Lisbeth's a very fussy eater," Mama would say. "She won't eat a thing unless you roll her food into little balls and sling them across the floor for her to chase."

It was a great shock to Lisbeth when she came to live with us. I don't chase kitties around the yard, and I CERTAINLY don't roll their food for them. (Besides dry food doesn't roll real well.)

But I was sure the move to "Cat Loving Kentucky" was going to be *wonderful* for us all, and, indeed, everything went well until the advent of *THE MOUSE*.

I opened a kitchen drawer one day in time for a small fuzzy creature to run across my hand and jump into the drawer below.

"Quick, Lisbeth," I grabbed the cat, figuring it was time for Lisbeth to earn her keep! "Look! A mouse! SIC EM!"

I dangled Lisbeth over the drawer where the mouse sat cowering in a corner. (It obviously didn't know Lisbeth well!)

"Go to it, Lizbeth!" I stuck her nose in the drawer. "Kill, kill!" I encouraged, but Lisbeth was not exactly riled up.

"Kill that thing? Why?" She looked up at me in that supercilious New Yorky type way. Her eyes spoke volumes!

"I don't DO mice! Thank you!"

Liz jumped to the floor and proceeded to wash her paws and to dab delicately behind the back of her ears. "MICE INDEED! Not even canned! Not even rolled into little balls for me to run after! Ha!"

Well, I got me some sturdy mouse traps at the K-Mart. With them I caught my finger, Lisbeth's fuzzy tail, and one small mouse (Bill disposed of the body of the small mouse.)

It was an exciting adventure (expecially Lisbeth's tail experience! But that's another story.) Lisbeth will just have to learn about Kentucky! There are lots of woods here, populated with lots of mice some of whom are going to enter our house now and then.

I don't like mice in my house! And if Lisbeth can't catch the occasional mouse for me, I'm going to have to take other measures. I'm going to get me a genuine *Kentucky* cat. They must be outstanding mousers! After all, everybody says:

"How 'bout them cats!"

Jane Hallock Combs

A Chat with Father Time

Last July 3rd, when I got home from the Choral Union rehearsal for our Fourth of July "Freedom Fest", there was a message on my answering machine. It was Papa Time. (We' re old buddies ... on familiar terms.)

"Hey, kid," he said, "Just wanted to wish you Happy New Year. Gotta run..." He hung up. I listened ... in puzzlement to the empty stactic on the machine. Then I dialed his number. After a few busy signals, I got through.

"Hey, Papa Time," I said. "Are you losing it or something? I got your message, but it's not New Year's Eve. Tonight's July 3rd. Tomorrow's the Big Bang at Roy Stewart stadium. It's going to be great. Hope you and the Mrs. are coming."

"Sorry, hon," he said. "It's the new schedule. Everything in life's gotten so speeded up lately, upper management decided we'd better go to a

258

new and shorter year... sort of update things. All the world's in a hurry. We've got to keep in step. Mustn't fall behind. So 'Happy New Year'.

"But wait," I said, "if this is New Year, what about the Fourth of July, Halloween, Thanksgiving, and Christmas? We can't just ignore them. You know what happened to Scrooge when he ignored Christmas..." I was mentally preparing myself for ghostly visitations.

"No problem," Papa Time was warming up to his theme. "With the new and improved year, we'll just have Christmas and the other biggies every *alternate* year. People can't afford all that expense anyway so there you have it."

"But you can't DO that!" I stammered.

"It's a done deal!" Papa Time's voice was sounding irritable. "Hadn't you noticed how fast this year has been moving along?"

"Well yes, I did wonder why the Fourth of July was following so quickly after Saint Patrick's Day."

"It's the new and improved rapid deployment of years. It's going to speed everything up. That way we can get all the political and personal problems out of the way quicker."

"Well, that's great," I said, "But what about the Freedom Fest? (I was hung up on the Fourth of July ... we'd been practicing for a long time getting ready for it. The Choral Union really sounded good!)

"Don"t worry about that. It was scheduled to be rained out anyway. You couldn't have sung if you wanted to.

"Listen," Papa Time's voice was getting decidedly edgy, "I've got to run now. We've got a big meeting in a few minutes ... February 22nd to be exact."

"February 22 is in a few minutes?"

"Are you dense? Think *new upgraded calender*. February is due any second now. You'll have to get used to all these new and exciting changes."

"But..." I stammered.

"No 'buts' Babe! Get with the program! Everything in life is speeded up. Microwaves, e. mail, the Information Highway. Time can't be an exception."

"But Papa Time … about the Fourth of July…"

"It'll be the new, improved Fourth of July a week from next Tuesday…"

"But…"

"If you have any other questions, after tomorrow you can drop me a note by E-Mail."

"You're going on-line?"

"Sure, isn't everyone? Gotta run, Babe. My E-dress is www. mytimebetterbeyourtime.com. Bye!"

And that's the scoop. I thought this year had had been moving a teensy bit fast.

Well, Happy Fourth of … I mean Happy New Improved New Year!

God Bless America

Murray State University's Choral Union folks are warming up their collective vocal cords getting ready for the Fourth. I sing with them. They probably wish I didn't, but I do. Every year we sing at the Roy Stewart Stadium, right before the fireworks.

In the autumn and Spring the Choral Union sings Mozart, Shubert, Brahmns and the like. But in the summer ... for the Fourth ... we sing lighter things: folk songs, Broadway show tunes, and ... of course patriotic songs.

Après nous comes the deluge of fireworks. It's exciting and fun to be part of the celebration. However, this year we're going to be singing "God Bless America". I hope I don't cry. It's a great song. I remember Kate Smith belting it out. I remember the time when there was a great hue and cry to make it our national anthem ... replacing the Star spangled Banner.

When we were practicing, It came back to me slowly ... the power of these songs. When we sing the words of the National Anthem it takes us back to the United States of the 1800's ... the rockets red glare ... the bombs..." Waiting to see if the flag was still there ... and the "dawn's early light" showing it was. Our anthem gives us history and a code passed down through generations. I love it. I wouldn't change it for anything.

Why would anyone have wanted to switch anthems? When the choral Union started practicing "God Bless America", I realized why. Sure, it was just another great, patriotic song until we got to the verse: "while the storm clouds gather, far across the sea, let us swear allegiance to a land that's free..." Memories came flooding back.

I remembered playing *God Bless America* on my piano when I was a girl. My piano teacher,

Miss Blanc, was an older, jewish lady with a strong, German accent. She had escaped from Germany just as the Jews were beginning to be rounded up. She was the only one of her large family that made it out. I remember that when Miss Blanc came for my piano lesson, often she would burst into tears. (It wasn't my playing, though I thought so at first.)

My mother would take Miss Blanc into the kitchen for tea and cookies while I practiced my Czerny. I would hear Miss Blanc's quietly sobbing voice as my mother spoke comforting words, and I tried to lose myself in arpegghios.

The news from Miss Blanc's family grew worse and worse. The letters were fewer ... fewer ... then no more letters came. Ever again!

I can see Miss Blanc now... her hands gnarled and crippled from arthritus. A student of a student of Liszt's, she left me with a love of the Romantics. I adored my piano lessons ... when Miss Blanc wasn't crying.

But the storm clouds gathered far across the sea ... and touched all our lives ... even the young. We had a bunch of kids that lived in our neighborhood. In the evenings we'd play "hide and seek" and "kick the can."

Some times the "big kids" would join us.

"Zip" Zipfield was a senior in high school. He and a couple of his friends would "hide and seek" with the 'little kids' just for fun. My young Uncle Dave, also a friend of Zip's, would be there too ... running and laughing in the warm twilight of a summer's evening.

But the war clouds continued to gather. Zip couldn't wait to be old enough to join the airforce. He went to Canada and joined the RAF. He learned to fly Spitfires. His plane went down in the English Channel. He was an only son. His parents never recovered from their loss.

And my "Unc"... my handsome, red haired Uncle Dave who loved hunting and fishing and a girl named Helen ... joined the U.S. Airforce the day after Japan bombed Pearl Harbor. He made it almost to the end of the war, but two weeks after he and Helen were married, he was killed. He was my grandparents only son … our only "Unc".

I remember sitting at the piano playing "From the mountains to the prairies to the oceans white with foam…" I remember not being able to see the music because of my tears. I couldn't play it after that.

I don't think I'll cry when we sing it on the Fourth of July, but I'm sure I'll be misty eyed. It's a powerful song with a lot of meaning for anyone who remembers that terrible time "when the war clouds gathered…"

The Glorious Fourth

The Glorious Fourth. Our Independance day. Always a special time for me. Our family fought on both sides of the Revolution. My mother's family ... English and Scottish ... wore redcoats I'm sure.

Dad's family, American back to 1640, had both loyalists and patriots counted among them. Capt. William Hallock sailed one of the first American "Naval" vessels. Actually it was a picket boat patrolling Long Island Sound during the Revolution. Long Island was a loyalist stronghold.

Our geneology states that Capt. William "suffered much from the British." I wonder if any of those "British" from whom he "suffered much" were my mom's people.

One of my other ancestors, John Washburn, a boy of 15, was left alone tending the family farm for a year in Westchester County, New York while the rest of his family, loyalists, fled to Long Island. Later, sick and alone John made his way through patriot lines to join his family on Long Island. Feverish and in a stupor he collapsed near the Sound, but was rescued by a black man who rowed him across the water and took him to the home of a French Huguenot family who nursed him back to health. I wonder if they had had to dodge Capt. Williams' picket boat as they made their way across the rough waters of Long Island Sound.

Phoebe and Rueben Wright, two of my patriot ancestors, at whose home Washington had spent five days and nights, were tortured by the Hessians who thought the Wrights might know some of Washington's plans. They didn't. I have some of Phoebe and Rueben's old coin silver spoons which had been buried in the yard when it was learned that the Hessians were coming. I cherish those spoons ... as I do the pitcher which is all that remains of the wash set that had been in the Wright's 'Guest room' and used by Washington.

The birth of freedom for this our Country was a long and arduous one ... a painful birth without benefit of Epidural.

I admire the strength and boldness of the people who stood up for what they believed in and were unafraid ... or if they were afraid, plowed right through it anyway and left us with this country which with all its faults and failings is still one of the last, best hopes in the world.

A few years ago, I was in New York with my mother visiting my brother Dave's family over the Fourth. The Fourth in Westchester can be pretty noisy. My mother, in her 80's, went to bed early before the fireworks really got warmed up. At the height of the sound of fire crackers bursting around the neighborhood, Mama woke up calling, "What was that, what was that?" She came to the head of the stairs, clearly frightened.

My fourteen year old nephew, Charlie, ran up the steps to comfort her.

"It's all right, Grandma," he said. "It's only fireworks! It's the Fourth of July!"

"Oh," my mother said, "I thought it was someone breaking in with guns!"

"No, no, Grandma," Charlie comforted, "It's OK"

"I was so worried!" My mother put her arm around Charlie. "I was worried about you and your Mama, and your daddy..."

"And Aunt Jane ... you were worried about Aunt Jane too..." I smiled as Charlie included me among the potential "victims". He's a sensitive kid.

I was a little shocked when my dear Momma said, "Oh no. Aunt Jane can take care of herself."

I was hurt at first, then decided it was a distinct compliment. I've always been pretty independent maybe I do have some genes of those patriots ... yes and loyalists ... and

Redcoats too who helped make our country what it is.

Jane Hallock Combs

Silver Spoons

Holiday season. Time to clean the antique silver. It's a routine. A hang over from the days when women did spring and fall cleaning. I am not into heavy housework. But before each holiday I *do* clean the silver. Not the sterling! Not all the stuff I got as wedding presents a million years ago. Not the things that sit dark and dingy like space debris in the bottom of the hutch. I clean the *antique* silver, the coin silver … the silver that connects me to the women I've heard about all my life … the women of my family.

The silver came to me from my grandma, the grandma who made huge, marvelous cookies called "Balovers". Grandma and I drank countless cups of tea together (mine heavily laced with milk and sugar when I was small).

I would stir the sugar lumps, with a fine coin silver spoon, round and round in one of

Grandma's fragile, bone china cups. While we'd sip our tea and munch Balovers...lots of Balovers ... Grandma would tell me the history of the spoons.

I think of that history now as I clean the same spoons in my modern, cluttered kitchen. The blackened surfaces of the spoons turn bright gradually, as the engraved initials begin to appear. The sun shines in through the window.

I twist the polished handle in the sun to better see the initials. "L.T."!

Letty Teed. I'd always liked the name. I don't know much about Letty, but I know where she is buried.

Grandma was a great cemetary walker. We walked miles together through family plots, Grandma reading the names and telling the histories, while I picked wild flowers. There were lots of daisies in the Teed plot.

I have six of Letty's spoons ... four delicate teaspoons and two huge, serving spoons.

What were you to me, Letty? Were you a great-great grandma? A great-great *Aunt*? What? Did you like to dance? Did you sing? Did you like your name? Grandma knew about you. She told me, but I've forgotten. I was too busy picking daisies or eating cookies! Sorry.

I clean another spoon. The letters "M.A.B." slowly peer out at me. Mary Anne Bertine, one of my Grandma's Great Grandmas ... decended from the French Huguenots.

In my youth, I always pictured her as a glamourous woman speaking with a lilting, French accent. A daguerreotype shows a fat, old lady in voluminous petticoats with a grim look on her face. Another fantasy flops. I grin as I polish the M.A.B. spoon thinking maybe in her youth, when these spoons were new, she *was* the slim, laughing girl of my fancy. Who knows? The spoons themselves show imagination. The initials are full of curlicues and fanciwork. I polish them and sing a little French song I learned in high school. My French isn't good. Ditto the song. Adieu Mary Anne! Adieu!

I fish around in the sudsy water and find the spoons that facinated me most as a child. They are the only ones that have a full first name (plus last initial). That name was … and is … mine!.

The smallest and most delicate of all the coin silver, the "Jane H." spoons belonged to my grandfather's grandmother. A quaker lady who always spoke using "thee" and "thou", Jane H. and her husband had been active in the Underground Railroad during the Civil War. Her house had a secret room where run-away slaves hid. I look at the spoons and wonder, did a black woman finding sanctuary in a home in Westchester, N.Y. ever share a cup of tea with Great-Great Grandma Jane? Did she ever stir her sugar into a tea cup with one of these spoons? Possibly with the one I now held in my hand? I polish it gently until it gleams.

I have a picture of that quaker Jane Hallock. In it she is an elderly lady wearing a lace cap on her head. Her face is sweet. She smiles. Jane H. lived to be 98. Did I inherit any of your genes, Grannie Jane?

I have your name, would I ever have had your courage? Will I have your years ... and that smile? I don't know.

The water in the sink is getting cool and dirty, but the last spoons I come to are the most special. The "P.W." spoons! The "buried" spoons! They had belonged to Jane H.'s grandmother, Phoebe Wright. Jane got her guts honestly. I polish the P.W. spoons thinking of Phoebe and The Revolution. Phoebe and her husband, Reuben, were newlyweds, 19 and 20. They were running a small Inn in Amawalk, New York when the fighting with the British broke out.

The Inn was in a strategic location as the American troops passed though Westchester. Several times George Washington stayed at

Wright's Inn. Once he stayed long enough to make the British think that possibly Phoebe and Reuben Wright had been privie to some of Washington's plans.

Phoebe's coin silver spoons and her other valuables had been buried in the back yard of the Inn when word came that the Hessians were en route to "question" the young couple. The Hessians questioned them all right! They burned the soles of their feet with hot coals from the fireplace trying to get them to divulge Washington's plans. Whether or not they knew anything, Phoebe and Reuben said nothing to the Hessians.

Long after the war, George Washington sent the Wright's a bowl with the presidential seal on it. He sent a letter, too, thanking them for their bravery. The bowl came down in our family as far as my favorite Grandmother. It's now in a museum in Yonkers. I remember Grandma taking me to see it once. I'd like to see it again, but for now I polish Phoebe's spoons.

I give an extra shine to the last spoon, then put all the coin silver back in the wooden spoon rack. The spoons glow softly in the sunlight, but it's time for me to stop remembering the past, and to get to work on today!

I put a tea bag into my cheery "World's Greatest Grandma" mug. I grab up a stainless steel spoon. I love my silly "Grandma" mug. This morning, though, after my involvement with the coin silver, the mug my grandson gave me looks so functional. The steel spoon seems cold and impersonal.

In the hutch is a Lennox cup and saucer I bought last week at an antique shop. I transfer the tea bag into the lovely cream-colored, bone china cup.

The water steams fragrantly as I fill the cup. I inhale the aroma luxuriously, then put one of

Phoebe's spoons on the saucer and carry it with me gently into my office.

Jane Hallock Combs

The Importance of a Second Language

You know the story of the mother cat who was out walking her kittens when they ran into a big, fierce-looking dog?

Tucking her kittens behind her, the mother cat opened her mouth and let out a series of bone chilling barks. As the terrified dog ran away, the mother cat turned to her kittens saying,

"Now do you see the advantage of speaking a second language?"

A second language is great, especially if you live with kids or animals.

I don't like swearing, particularly not at kids, but Spanish has always been handy for me when those near and dear push me to the limit or beyond.

"Cállate la boca grande," has always been more effective than plain "shut-up!" (which I don't care for either).

But sometimes words aren't enough. You must take action especially when dealing with animals.

I found during Sam's puppyhood that he hated it if I dropped anything on the floor. He'd pick it up and bring it to me (he IS a retriever.)

Also, if an envelope or piece of paper protruded from the edge of the coffee table, he would bring IT to me, suggesting I put it in its proper place. (What a NAG HE IS!)

I took atvantage of this behavior to train Sam. I took a blank envelope and wrote on it, "Please, I need to go BAD! NOW!" I put the envelope on my coffee table with the end of it sticking out where Sam could easily see it. Whenever he brought it to me, I looked at it with wide eyes and said, "Oh you want to go out?" Then I'd open the front door.

After only a couple of times, Sam got the idea. After a while, I stopped messing with the deliberately left envelope. Today, if Sam has any difficulty getting my attention when he needs to go out, he'll go to my waste paper basket, retrieve an envelope, bringing it to me with a pleading look in his eyes.

Animals are not verbal, but they're certainly not dumb! They're creatures of body language and action.

My friend, Kate, had a cat named "Dum, Dum" who learned how to bounce a ball.

"Tapoca, tapoca, tapoca". Dum-Dums's little red ball would bounce up and down on the wooden floors. Interesting conversation piece. Cute! During the day. Not as cute at night.

One rainy night, Kate and her love were snuggled down under the quilts while the rain pattered on the skylight of the roof above. They slept that wonderful rain induced sleep of the angels with their huge, black Lab, Brookie curled cozily at the bottom of the bed until:

"Tapoca, tapoca, tapoca!" Clever "Dum-Dum" the cat began her bouncing routine two inches from their bed.

Coming groggily up from the veil of sleep, Kate became aware of the cat's performance. But she was too far gone to try to stop it. Her husband was aware of the show too. Kate heard low growls from the other side of the bed, but neither one of them was making a move to intercept the cat. And then the dog, Brookie, raised his shaggy head. Kate could feel him stir:

"Tapoca, tapoca, tapoca". The ball bounced on...then:

"Tapoca, tapoca, taPOC!..." after that ... nothing. Silence.

Brookie had leaned off the bed and snagged the ball in mid bounce. Back to wonderful sleep.

The next morning, Kate found the red ball tucked under a blanket at the bottom of the bed.

It's good to speak "animaleze" and to communicate with them, but sometimes words fail and actions need to be taken.

Brookie is a dog of action...and definitely not a "dum-dum"!!

Shakespeare, Dogs and Filthy Beasts

Dogs are so enthusiastic! Big dogs are especially enthusiastic! Big, dirty dogs with wet, muddy paws are by far the most enthusiastic!

Shakespeare and I have a lot in common when we view the whole dog situation.

Whoever said, "The dog is man's best friend" wasn't Shakespeare, I'm pretty sure, and I know it wasn't me! Whoever did say it was not really being politically incorrect. The DOG is not "Woman's best friend."

What woman in her right mind craves a best friend who slobbers all over her, festoons her wardrobe with shedded hair, and smells up the entire house (the part of the house which is left over after said dog finishes his "teething" routine)?

Now I'm not talking about Chihuahuas, Shih-Tzus, Poodles or any of those cute, fuzzy little dogs, those decorative cuddlers who are more like retarded cats than *dogs!!* Some of THEM may be termed "Woman's best friend", I suppose, But they are not DOGS really, are they? That's just a scam.

By the term *DOG*, I am thinking of German Shepherds, Rottweilers and their ilk, but most especially I'm, thinking ... of necessity ... I'm thinking, of America's current number one favorite, the Laborador Retriever, or as my son used to refer to them, "Lavatory Retrievers." Actually that's a very apt name since DOGS do have some nasty personal habits like drinking from the "you know what." Though my own least favorite thing is the way dogs think that the cat's litter box is where their "little snacks" are stored. The cat doesn't think a whole lot of that either. (*Dog owner's rule #1: Never kiss a dog with Kitty Litter hanging from his whiskers*).

My husband and I are owned by a gigantic yellow lab named Samson. Samson, or "Sam" as he's known to his friends and intimates (better be his friend and intimate or he'll knock you down, sit on your chest and lick your face until you claim "buddyship" with him. Sam's very friendly!)

Anyway, Sam caught Bill and me in a weak moment when he was a pup...a HUGE pup! A huge pup with big, brown imploring eyes. (*Rule #2: Ignore any pup with imploring eyes ...* Better yet, ignore pups totally ... the little buggers get you hooked, then when you turn around, they've turned into DOGS. There's not a whole lot you can do about it ... particularly because by that time, your husband will have bonded with the beast and there you are ..."Man's best friend!" Filthy beast and buddy),

I'll always be more of a cat person than a dog fan, and for that reason I've always felt a special kinship with Will Shakespeare. After all, he didn't think a whole lot of dogs either. I know. I studied Shakespeare in college. He didn't talk about dogs a lot and what he *does* say is mostly not good. My favorite quote, the one that sticks with me, is from *Macbeth* where he has Mrs. Macbeth summing the whole thing up when she says that immortal line:

"Out, out, DAMMED SPOT!"

Mixed Marriages

Mother told me to avoid a mixed marriage. Bad stuff, you know. Confused kids, hostile neighbors, family friction. Black/white, oriental/caucasion, religious/non, it's all the same. Marital troubles!

But, what happens when a sweet, simple girl from New York marries a 6'4" Kentucky boy? As Crocodile Dundee would say, "Now *THAT'S a mixed marriage!*"

He's right! Think about it. Not only is there the background and cultural problems, there's the REAL problem … the *language barrier!*

My family thinks Bill talks funny! Personally, I love that wonderful, sexy, Kentucky twang. It makes my toes curl. Love it!

The big man, for his part, is addicted to my New Yorky pronunciation of "winter" (with a clearly sounded "T" as apposed to his Southern

"Winnah.") Since we lived our first married years in Florida, the term "winter" didn't come up a lot. I sort of had to force it into conversations a bit, like:

"Have you noticed it's not quite as hot *this* winTer as it was *last* winTer?

Or...

""There's never a good *winTer* around when you need one."

Or...

"Do you catch much crappie in Kentucky in the *winTer?*"...

(I wasn't certain what "crappie" was, but I knew Bill liked eating it and probably had hunted it often in his Kentucky youth.)

No, the language barrier didn't appear to be a problem at first. Then it raised its ugly head. It all started innocently enough. I had splurged and blown half of my grocery budget on a huge beef roast for the two of us. We were almost through a delicious, candle-lit dinner when Bill twanged out at me:

"Boy, this sure would make some fine tasting hash!"

"Hash?" I asked.

"Hash!"

I had always hated hash with a passion. My mother used to make it all the time when I was a kid.

"You really *LIKE* hash?" I asked my beloved.

"Like it? I LOVE it!"

The next day, Bill asked me if I planned to use the rest of the roast for hash. I choked thinking of that lovely, rare, roast beef that I could slice for sandwiches or use in a bunch of creative New Yorkish-type ways. But like a good newly-wed I said, "Well, maybe!" (When in doubt, always equivocate.)

I made myself a roast beef sandwich to take to work and relegated the hash to the darker corner of my mind until later.

On the drive home, visions of my mother's hash danced in my head. (Not a dance exactly ... more of a blind stagger. Only things you LIKE "dance" in your head!)

Mama had always made her hash with corned beef, but if Bill's mom had used roast beef, I guessed it could be done.

I got home and, with anguish, took that great roast and ground it into a mess of meat lumps. I added onions and potatoes and began to cook the daylights out of it in my largest skillet, turning the mass as it browned.

By the time Bill walked in, we had a huge skillet full of New York style hash.

Bill looked at it and asked:

"What the *WORLD* is that stuff?"

"Hash!" I answered sounding naturally miffed.

"That's not hash!"

"Is too, is too!" (I reverted to the ultimate argument ploy.)

"Hash is juicy! That stuff's all dried out, half burned!" Bill retaliated. He poked at the mess.

"Hash is supposed to be dried out, half burned, and totally disgusting!" I knew my hash!

Later, after Bill had sworn he'd be hung by his hair before he'd eat so much as a spoonful of that mess, and I had confessed that I'd never eaten "hash" without a stomach pump handy, we cried (over the lovely roast wasted and over the cat's rejection of a plate filled with hash just for her ... the ultimate insult!) Then Bill explained that "Kentucky" hash was made with lots of left over gravy, meat cut into nice, little, rectangular chunks (not ground) with onions and potatoes happily swimming around with the meat in the bubbling juice.

"But that's not 'Hash'," I shouted, sadness turning to joy! "That's 'Goop!'" (one of my all time favorite left-over dishes from my teen years. Goop! Glorious Goop!)

It's all in the language ... connotation and denotation ... things like that. These days, after a beef roast, we often have HASH/GOOP and everyone is happy. Even the cat!

Retrievers and Dead Ducks

The other day I read that constant picking at ones clothes can be an early sign of Alzheimer's. More likely dog ownership. "Ownership"... an interesting term.

Bill and I are owned by Sam, the yellow Lab. He got us one day, two years ago. We had been sitting on our front porch when this befuddled looking puppy came wandering down the dirt road that stretches away for miles beyond our home. When the pup reached our drive, tongue hanging out, a look of abandoned panic in his eyes, Bill called out:

"Hey, puppy, where're you going?"

With that, the pup turned, grinned, and bounded up our driveway, onto our porch, and into our hearts and souls.

"I'm Sam," he said. "Been looking for you!"

I've been picking at dog hairs ever since.

Sam had no collar nor any identification on him. All he had was a nasty, skinned place on his nose which was probably, according to the vet, the result of "having been thrown from a car."

We called the Humane Society and checked newspapers for a couple of weeks to see if anyone had "lost" Sam. When no one claimed ownership, Sam was ours, and we were his.

Retrievers are splendid dogs, but they ARE "retrievers." A desire to be helpful and to carry things for their people is bred into them. Deeply! Retrievers MUST help! Swell for carrying dead ducks and stuff.

We don't have a whole lot of dead ducks lying around the house, so Sam, now an adult retriever, has to make do helping where and when he can.

When Bill retrieves the garbage can, Sam retrieves the lid carrying it like a shield before him, head held high filled with the pride of WORK! Talk about your "work ethic." Labs invented it!

The Color Chartreuse, Etc.

In the house, Sam follows me around waiting to be of service. I empty the waste baskets. He grabs the empty basket and returns it to its place. If it's one of the bigger baskets, Sam lifts his head, the rim of the basket covering his face, totally obscuring his view. No matter! Sam knows to which room the basket belongs. Off he goes, bumping into walls and furniture en route to the basket place. It's a challenge!

Doing laundry with a retriever at your side is a challenge too. When I attempt to carry a load of clothes to the laundry, Sam is beside me grabbing stuff out of my hands. Sam believes towels and washcloths are totally his responsibility. He brings them to me one at a time. He, naturally, has to shake them … HARD … to make sure they're dead … before bringing them to me. With each towel and wash cloth we have to have a discussion about dropping, and just who's in charge of the laundry around here anyway! The

297

laundry process is a lengthy one. My towels all are very dead.

If WASHING is hard, I really have to slip around hiding the clothes after they have come *out* of the dryer.

"I'll hep! I'll hep!" His gapping mouth grabs at the clean sheets while I do my African tribesman imitation, balancing the load on top of my head. I stagger down the hall with Sam trying to reach at least a clean shirt or two. He such a GRABBER!

Sam grabs and carries my purse when I come into the house. He MUST grab it! It's his JOB! (ANOTHER ONE!) With the straps dangling around his knees, he lugs my purse in his wet, slobbering mouth while prancing towards the closet. All my purses have slobber marks on them. They match my clothes. I am a lovely sight. People comment.

I think Sam may have been a purse snatcher in a previous existence. Or a dancer.

My elderly neighbor uses a cane. Sam likes to carry it for her. He snatches it from her hands at a dead run then dances around with it in his mouth looking for all the world like Fred Astaire. All he needs is a top hat. Everyone thinks it's a riot (except for my neighbor who can't see much from her vantage point sprawled face down in the daffodils).

Sam's a wonderful dog and a vital part of our life. But this retrieving instinct can be a pain!

I'd like to tell you more, but I've got to pick some dog hair off my slacks, get my neighbor up out of the daffodils again, and then I think I'll go and buy me a couple of dead ducks.

Survival of the Funniest

Kentuckians, especially *West* Kentuckians, are a rare breed of survivors ... rare and funny. Their unquenchable sense of humor had a lot to do with that survival.

Descendants of tough folks who scrambled through dense woods, over treacherous mountain passes to get into the fabled "land of Kentucke", today's West Kentuckians show their Anglo/Irish/Scottish heritage not only by their looks, (check all the redheads and strawberry blonds around) but by their laughter.

The pioneers brought with them their laughter ... and their hair... (if the Cherokees didn't see and covet it). They brought everything they owned, (everything that a woman or mule could carry...the men were busy lugging their rifles and concentrating on catching lunch). When not looking for rabbit and squirrel for stew, the men were busy fending off unfriendly types ... bears, wild cats, scalp collectors, and New Yorkers (the latter two often thought to be synonymous).

Sometimes they (woman or mule with occasional assist from happy, hunter hubby) dragged a cart after them ... but without much more than an old path to toodle along on, carts and the luxuries contained therein (clocks, bedding, Grannie's fruitcake pan) were dropped by the wayside while Mama hoisted the flour and suger sacks up on to a hip that was unoccupied (except for the twins who had to shove over a bit.)

We all know about the law of the "survival of the fittest". Check around West Kentucky ... in Paducah, Benton, Mayfield ... anywhere along "The Purchase." Look at those big, rugged, handsome men and ditto women. Survivors! Sons and daughters of survivors!

The strength of the women is not, at first glance, as obvious as the men's ... but talk about your "Steel Magnolias" (the women, not the men). They grow around here like weeds! Strong, good looking, tough folks all!

Kentuckians have a lot of interesting personal characteristics, but one trait they all have in common is their FANTASTIC sense of humor.

Why humor? Why is it so endemic (in Western Kentucky particularly)? Think about it.

The early pioneers had few material possessions, and to say their lives were extremely hard is a gross understatement. The further West you went, the harder it became. Pioneer life killed off all those who had any trace of weakness. Cravings for fast foods or warm houses or just a propensity for the sniffles could do you in pretty quick!

Heading West, the pioneers dropped off their extraneous stuff. If something wouldn't last for the long haul, out it went! (Unfortunately true for the occasional wife and child too). Wimpy husbands didn't even *attempt* to start out … that's why the few you find in West Kentucky now must, of course, be later imports.

Mental baggage was something else dumped along the wooded trail with mad abandon. How many Kentuckians do you know who are slobbering sentimentalists? Few. Sentimentality does not travel real well. It went out right after Grannie's fruitcake pan.

But humor is a sustaining thing! Humor was lugged along even when the pioneers got down to nothing. I mean NADA!

I can see it now:

"Pa, what happened to the twins?"

"Darned if I know, ma! Last saw them when we were scrambling over that ole' mountain back there where I shot the big ba'r."

"What do you think we ought to do, Pa?"

"I don't know … Want to hear a funny story?"

You know all of the studies done on the therapeutic value of humor? I believe West Kentuckians were among the first examples.

(History books usually comment on the Kentuckian's general good humor and great joy in laughter). It's been proven that laughter starts endorphins flowing all over the place. Endorphins perk you up pretty quick. The pioneers triggered up bunches of endorphines proving that the survival edge could be achieved through laughter.

When you wander into a West Kentucky restaurant today, don't expect great outpourings of sloppy sentimentality or a whole lot of fruitcake, but do be prepared to stumble over endorphins. They bound around the place and cause people to wear genuine, warm, smiley faces. Be prepared for honest good feelings and laughter that reverberates through a room, bounces off the walls and echoes through the hills and across the corn fields. Respect it! It has the potential power to sustain.

Oh! And the twins caught up with Ma and Pa just in time to catch Pa's punch line.

Pioneers and Settlers

Pioneers and Settlers. They're different. It probably hasn't kept you up nights thinking about it, unless you're one type or the other married (or cohabiting) with someone of the opposite persuasion, but, they are different!

I speak from experience.

My family, settlers all, arrived from England in 1640. (Must have been big trouble with the king, church, or *somebody*, because Hallocks don't move across the street easily … let alone across an ocean.) Hallocks arrived in Long Island, settled down (what settlers do best), and have scarcely moved since.

My husband's family, though, are pure bred, dyed-in-the-sheep Pioneers. The Combses bounded off the boat in New Jersey shortly after the Hallocks plopped down in Long Island. They took one look at Jersey and left.

They spent a week and a half in Maryland, (checking out the squirrel and bear populations), then zipped into Virginia whacking down trees and, marking trails as they went. (Not that they ever planned to head back...but because Combses are natural born tree whackers and trail blazers.)

The Combs boys, nine of them, made it into Virginia where they stayed long enough to produce large batches of offspring. Then they split up and headed out for different parts of West Virginia, Kentucky and points beyond, intent on finding newer lands, fatter squirrels, and bigger, better, basketball teams.

When I, descendant of a long line of happy Hallock settlers, married Bill Combs, scion of the Combs pioneer clan, I hadn't given much thought to our basic differences. They are there. There are the obvious things like his wanting to move every six months and my wanting to stay in one place until I mildew. Then there are the subtler things like shopping.

If I mention we need a loaf of bread, Bill is up and has his jacket on saying, "Let's go!" while I'm trying to decide on white or rye. He holds the door:

"I thought you meant we were going TODAY!"

It's the pioneer in him. In the back of his mind he is always thinking about leaping up and tracking down food.

"I meant we need bread next time we go shopping."

"If you need it, we'd better get it." He's outside warming up the car while I'm thinking about what else we could use at the store since we are obviously headed that way.

Shopping is a whole new experience. Especially shopping en masse with my female in-laws. Pioneers all, they attack shopping the way General Patton attacked the enemy during WW II. Break through the lines and create havoc in the rear! Whack down trees! Get in and get out! Fast!

The first time I went shopping with "Mama Combs" and my two "sisters-in-law." I remember getting a shopping cart. As I unfolded my neat list, I saw, out of the corner of my eye, Mother Ruth roaring off down the center aisle in command of another cart with "the girls," Teddy Lou and Susie, heading off in opposite directions *obviously* intent on surrounding the market. (And taking the manager hostage?) I looked up again. They had all disappeared!

I started off, shouting:

"Wait for me, I've got the list!"

But I could only see flashes of "the girls" as they swept past the ends of aisles (in coordination with Ruth who, like a white haired bulldozer, plowed her cart through the frozen food section). Teddy Lou and Susie ran past her in a fine, synchronized display, tossing heads of cabbage, packages of cheese and small pizzas into the speeding, shopping cart. Susie made a smooth hook shot with a cantaloupe that netted her at least three points.

About the time I had gotten to the fresh vegetable section and had carefully placed a small bunch of broccoli in my cart, they caught up with me.

"Guess we got about everything!" Their cart was overflowing. The cantaloupe bobbed merrily on top. They'd bought enough for a short trek to Wisconsin at least.

"We've decided to go home, stick this stuff in the fridge, cut down that old pine tree in the back yard, then head over to Paducah to the mall. Wanna go?"

Why not? Paducah wasn't anywhere *near* as far as Wisconsin, and I could hardly wait to see what your basic, pioneer-type woman could do to a mall!

Killer Cat

A killer lives at my house. She's little and dainty with a small nose and mouth that perfectly match the pink collar around her white neck. White, gray and pink. She's lovely, but she is a killer … and an Episcopalian!

You wouldn't expect that.

The kitty had been on her own for some time. She lived in St. John's Memorial Garden existing "paw to mouth" on whatever small creatures she could catch. She even caught (and ate!) a squirrel.

When folks at St. John's were not watching, she would slip into church for a bit of prayer and probably warmth (it was late winter).

I first saw her at an E.C.W. meeting when the Episcopal Church Women were working on preparing layettes for the hospital.

"What's that?" Kathy asked.

310

It was pouring rain outside and hard to hear the small meow from the sodden gray and white kitty hanging precariously by her front paws from the window (like the cat on the "Hang in there baby" cards and posters that were popular a while back).

"It's just that cat again!" Eve answered.

I let the little cat in, dried her off, and put down some milk for her. As she purred and lapped at the milk, I heard her story.

"I hadn't heard anything about that," I said, feeling left out.

"Well Jane," Marge looked over her glasses at me, "If you'd show up more often for Wednesday night service, you might know what was going on."

Evidently the previous Wednesday (also rainy), just as our vicar was starting to serve the Eucharist, everyone heard a pitiful meowing. It was the cat outside the St. Francis door that opens onto the memorial garden.

Kitty was intuitively at the right place. The St. Francis door, named for St. Francis of Assisi, has a stained glass window depicting the saint surrounded by his beloved little animals. How appropriate! How clever of the kitty!

That evening after the Ladies Layette business, I was back at St. John's for another meeting. It was still raining out.

As the bishop's committee sat in a circle around a table discussing the church's business and its future, once again appeared a sodden kitty hanging on the window as rain ran down her face.

Ben let her in, and after her acknowledging the Bishop's committee by rubbing wetly up against everyone, she ended up curled on my lap for the rest of the meeting, purring loudly.

I petted her, of course, and could feel all her bones just beneath the surface of her skin. This kitty had had a hard early life.

When the meeting ended, I had to take her home. I couldn't put her out into the rain again. Anyway, I had been thinking about getting a second cat. I'd been seeing traces of mouse in my garage lately, and the car's headlights had shown me a little rodent running across the garage floor just the previous day.

Since my elderly Persian, Lisbeth, doesn't DO mice, thank you, I needed a good mouser.

"You've got to call her Francis." The bishop's committee was in complete agreement for once. "Since she tried to get in the St. Francis door … it's perfect! It's the only name!"

I tried the name Francis on her and took her home. I don't think she'd been in a car before. She was excited by the lights. Most of the way home, she rode sitting on my shoulder staring out the window and purring in my ear.

The first two weeks she was with me, although I was feeding her lots of 9-Lives cat food, she was catching (and eating) at least two mice or moles a day.

It's been almost six months now since she's been living with us, a cute, funny little creature who follows Sam, the Lab and me on long walks. Cats don't usually do that. When Sam and I turn around to come home so does kitty. She comes too when I call her name. Even if she is off hunting in the field across the way, I can call her name and then see flashes of white as she bounds through the deep weeds heading home.

A marvelous mouser and a real killer, she still hunts though she no longer does it for survival. Now she's more of a "sports hunter", but it keeps the mice down.

Oh, and her name's different too. I looked at her one day and decided she was just really not a "Francis". She's a "Ceci." I think St. Francis would have liked that. I know he'd like Ceci.

Machosisimo

Some people think Kentucky men are macho. Well yes, perhaps some have leanings that way, but for the definition of machoism you need to look further south ... like Argentina.

I went there a few years ago with Granddaughter Melanie. We found out about macho men. We visited friends of mine, former students. It was fun, and educational!

The day after we arrived, our friends took us sight seeing in Buenos Aires.

Simple. You go to a sight. Get out. See it. Go on. Right? Wrong!

The first sight we got to, host Alejandro stopped the car and handed wife Mimi, out of the back seat while Melly and I popped out of the other doors. Whoops. Faux pas! Big! Mimi took me aside in the museum whispering that Melly and I should let Alex open the car doors for us.

"Eet hurts his feelings eef you do not! Eet ees, how you say, a macho theeng! He is strong and we are weak women."

From that moment on, getting out of the car became a bigger production than "Les Miserables." Going *ANYWHERE*, Mel and I would sit in our seats while Alejandro hopped out of the car, opened the left rear door, handed Mimi out, then dashed around to the passenger side, opened *my* door, handed *me* out, then to the right rear door hauling *Melly* out.

All lovely, courteous and ... SLOW! But it saved Alex's machismo. He was "beeg and strong." We were "little and weak" ... even though I towered over him and outweighed him by ten pounds!

Then there was the 'light' thing. After spending three days in Buenas Aires, Alejandro and Mimi drove us across the Pampas to their home 800 miles away. 800 miles sounds like a long trip, but actually we bounded across the unpaved road at a good clip. *A really good clip!* We made the 800 miles in slightly over eight hours including a stop at a cathedral! I spent a lot of time in the cathedral praying ... and tending to the blister rising up on my hand from the death grip I maintained on the door handle. When I mentioned to Alejandro that we "were certainly making good time," he assured me I shouldn't worry since he had been a race car driver in his youth. Somehow I had sensed that.

Mimi's only comment on our "making good time" was to express the hope "We'd get to San Juan before dark." The rate we were going, I figured we'd probably be there before tea-time. Then I noticed every twenty minutes or so Mimi would repeat her hope we'd "get to San Juan before dark."

She wasn't worried we were hurdling along a rough, gravel road on the Pampas at one hundred plus miles per, but she was afraid of the dark!

She said it again as I noticed the sun heading west … Winter in Argentina. The days short. Still a ways from San Juan, the sky turned purple, and the sun slid silently behind the Andes.

"I KNEW we wouldn't get there before the sun went down." The wild ride across the plains hadn't fazed her … but she had some kind of sun fetish. Wasn't that Mayan. Or Aztec?

Anyway, it was getting dark and our host, who never thought of slowing down his mad, bumping pace, had neglected to turn on his lights. How could I broach the subject to a macho Argentinean? "For heavens sake! Aren't you going to turn on your lights?" didn't strike me as quite right, so when a car came towards us without lights, I took the opportunity to say:

"Look at that idiot driving without his lights on!"

"I know," cried Mimi from the back seat. "Argentinean men hate to admit they can't see well at night so no one turns their lights on. I hate it!" I hated it a lot too!

Three minutes later, we spotted a fire in the road. Mimi begged Alejandro to slow down or at least turn on his headlights. But "NO!". We roared by a horse that had been run over. The fire marked the spot so others wouldn't follow suit. I saw tire marks across the animal as we flashed by.

The rest of the drive was relatively uneventful. We made it to San Juan, the city with the "highest accident rate in Argentina"! Alejandro seemed pleased with this achievement. The macho aversion to headlights had to be factor ... also the fact that traffic lights in San Juan are considered more decorative pieces than objects of traffic control). I don't know!

Is it a macho thing or does it have something to do with inherent "goodness" or lack thereof? I'd never thought about it until our last evening in San Juan when Alejandro observed that "Americans are so-o-o GOOD…"

"Good?" I asked.

"Yes … Americans are so good. They always stop at red lights!"

That told me something. It told me I'd be very glad to get back again to dear, GOOD, mildly macho, Kentucky … my home sweet home!

Shopping in the Argentine

Melly and I were in Buena Aires when the peso was VERY low compared to the dollar. Alejandro and Mimi, our hosts, wanted to take us shopping with their wealthy cousin whose closest friend was at that time the world's richest man. She often shopped with him.

I've always tried to make it a rule NEVER to shop with anyone who hobnobs with the world's richest man.

"Elena knows where the good bargains are!" my friends said. (This to a person whose idea of shopping excitement is catching a "Blue Light Special" at the K-Mart).

Under the best of conditions, I am not a shopper. When forced to upgrade my wardrobe, I make a bee line for the sale racks, grab *something* that will blend with my other stuff, is approximately the right size, then get the heck out of the store. "Shop til I drop" I don't.

"With the dollar strong now," my friends assured me, "there are many bargains".

I figured that my idea of bargains and fabulously wealthy peoples' might differ, but I did need a new pair of jeans, and maybe some tennis shoes. We shot off to The Patio Bullrich Shopping Center, a gorgeous place filled with designer boutiques overflowing with elegantly coiffed, magnificently dressed women who wouldn't know a K-mart if they fell over one. Great place for the young and reckless, not the middle aged and thrifty.

"Oh look!" I spotted a shoe store with some tennies in the window. White leather too!

"No, no, no!" My friends dragged me, wimpering, away. They then whisked me into a little boutique where ALL THE SHOES WERE HANDMADE! Handmade and *ugly!* I knew I was behind the times, but big, clunking heels and solid leather soles that won't bend unless you hit them with a hammer, have never appealed to me. The owner of the shop dragged out 165 pairs of shoes in my size. All incredibly well made. (Each stitch was pointed out to me by the owner and my three friends.)

"These shoes would cost $300 or $400 back in the States," they said.

Would that have made them look any nicer? I wondered. My friends all LOVED the shoes. It was embarrassing trying to work up excitement over all the ugliness.

"Well these aren't too awful" hardly sounds right! I finally ended up the owner of two pairs of shoes COMPLETELY HAND MADE. One pair … patent leather … looked like something Fred Astaire would wear to dance in. If I ever take up tap dancing and get me a tuxedo, I'm set!

The other pair is utility brown suede with big, brown buckles. They weren't as repulsive as some of the other shoes, and I have no strength of character. My fellow shoppers ADORED THEM. Could I continue to offend them by rejecting the shoes they persisted in shoving under my nose and over my toes?

"Look at these, Jane, how they are made! They will NEVER wear out!"

That's what I was afraid of.

"HAND MADE!" They said in chorus.

'Wow' I said.

With reluctant fingers I forked over the equivalent of $60 for the two pair of HAND MADE shoes which I may wear as a lark some day. (Is it tacky to wear a small, discrete sign that says, "These HANDMADE shoes would sell for $300 or $400 in the U.S"?).

But back to the shopping.

I did see a coat I adored in a store window. A light weight wool, perfect for Kentucky winters.

"No, no, no!" The anvil chorus started up again. "Not good enough for you".

They dragged me away from this sensible looking store and whipped me into a little designer outerwear emporium where skinny girls with big lips wandered around modeling the wares and the manager himself grabbed me and started draping a cape around me.

"Eet es so reech and stylesh! Perfect for fiestas or thee OPERA!"

I couldn't convince them that we didn't have many fiestas or operas in Western Kentucky. Before I knew it, we had walked out of the store with me in possession of a green, tweed cape 22 1/2 yards long. No strength of character!

It looks striking with my klutzy, patent leather dancing slippers. When I wear it, I position the huge shoulder pads somewhere in the right vicinity, then gather my strength and heave one end of the cape. It flies across my shoulder and maybe catches the other side. Occasionally, if the wind is right and my arm is in pitching form, the cape wraps around me two or three times. Of course, then I can barely walk. But never mind. I look so "reech and stylesh", people come from miles around to carry me.

Think of it this way, carried, I'll never dirty up my dancing slippers! I do worry a bit about how I'm going to leap into my little Subaru in the cape and charge off to The Piggly Wiggly on a cold winter day, but it looks like it's going to be a mild winter this year. I live in hope.

My Time of POWER

Life sometimes seems filled with scams large and small ... and brimming over with interesting inconsistancies. Like the other day:

I'd gone outside. The sun was shining. The sky was bluer than Paul Newman's eyes, but it was raining so hard six ducks had taken refuge in my garage!

I squinted up at the sun and muttered, "There's GOT to be a rainbow."

Sure there was a rainbow. The end of it was probably about to bop me on the head with a pot of gold any minute because ... after all ... I was in my TIME OF POWER!

Let me enlighten you about the *marvelous* thing that happened to me (and probably to a zillion others nationally).

I got an "URGENT" letter from a lady named Jay Peah who is the "Famous World Consultant" (that's what it says on her letterhead) who had come "halfway around the world from England to contact ME! I was impressed.

She claimed, modestly, to be "the world's #1 astrologer" who had made this trip "for the sole purpose of informing me that my Time of Power was coming up!"

Hey, wow! (I hadn't had a "Time of Power" since I was three and knew that if I got scared, lonely, bored or thirsty in the middle of a dark night, I could bang on the wall causing my papa to get up, stumble around in the dark and bring me a glass of water. (That "Power Time" had come to a screeching halt the night Papa stumbled the wrong way and fell down the stairs dislocating his back ... after that I was on my own water-wise).

But to get back to my current "Time of Power" ... Ms. Peah had found out about my coming "into it" through "the famed Astrological Association of England." Somehow those boys had looked up at the sky, and my name was written all across it. She says that "unique astrological influences had now set me apart from other people." (I HAD noticed people edging away from me lately. I thought it was bad breath. But what did I know?)

"For a very short time period … starting now," she said, I could "have the chance to acquire all the money I want! All the success I want! All the love and happiness I want!" WOW! (My husband likes the money, success and happiness parts, but says I've got enough love already, thank you!)

Not only does Ms. Peah say that I'll have all this good stuff, but she GUARANTEED that within the next 42 days (those astrological guys really have this down to a science now) I was going to amass over a MILLION DOLLARS!" Boy, oh boy! (Think of all the lottery tickets I could buy!)

Because of my fantastic potential, she had actually chosen "not to be working with the British Royal Family" for the next few weeks so she could devote herself exclusively to working with me. It was her "deepest desire" for me to "fulfill my potential for becoming a happy millionaire." Tears came to mine eyes. She was too kind!

There was absolutely "no obligation on my part because my "Time of Power had begun." Of course, she'd like me to send her $20 so that I might receive my own personal "Time of Power Action Plan" ... complete with "Good Fortune/Money instructions GUARANTEED TO BRING ME THE CHANCE TO ENJOY ONE MILLION DOLLARS DURING MY TIME OF POWER!" Golly gee!

I immediately sat down and wrote this darling lady the following reply:

"Dear Ms. Peah:

Thanks so much for letting me know about my marvelous good fortune! I am thrilled to pieces about it. And your coming "halfway around the world just to contact me" was SO nice! I do appreciate your kindness.

I'm a little short this week and can't send you the $20, but I don't foresee any real problem about that. Just send me your "power plan", and, when the money starts ROLLING in, I'll mail you off a check. Better than that, since you've been SO nice and have gone to so much trouble coming over here from England and all, maybe you'd be interested in investing in ME since I am in my TIME OF POWER and have so much potential!

If you would care to send me your check or money order for $100,000 by return mail, I will guarantee you ten percent of my income WHATEVER THAT MAY BE for the next … not 42 days … but for this ENTIRE YEAR!! Think of that, Ms. Peah. What an opportunity! What a chance of a lifetime! Let me hear from you soon."

I haven't heard anything back yet from "The World Consultant and #1 Astrological Expert", but I expect she is probably up to her starry eyes writing my "power plan". I think while I wait for the mailman to come, I'll go outside and check under the bushes for pots of gold.

Dust Bunnies of Spring

It's springtime. I can tell because my skin is all dried up and looks like a mummy's (of the Egyptian variety). Winter does that. By spring I'm a mess.

I've got some lotion that helps my skin look a tad more human, but unfortunately Sam (the yellow Lab) loves it. Sam tends to follow me around licking at the backs of my knees. It's a little distracting, especially if you are a writer trying to think deep, intellectual, philosophical thoughts. I don't believe Thoreau had a dog. Or else he had good skin.

So ... it's springtime. If I can't write deep, intellectual stuff, maybe I could at least clean my house. It looks pretty bad after the winter too. I'm not a housecleaning fanatic, at least not like my friend, Susan. I don't dust frogs.

Susan Up-The-Street (that's her location, not her cognomen) is a wonderful person. A good mother, a fine wife, an excellent nurse, and a neat, tidy person who tends to carry neatness to extremes.

Susan's putting a new office in her house. She's got a new computer and is, of course, building a room around it. She's thinking of putting in a hardwood floor. She'll set the floor off with a persianesque rug...

"Great," I said when she told me. "Wood floors and area rugs are really in now, but you realize that with wood floors you're going to get the occasional dust bunny under your furniture."

I remember cleaning my bedroom when I was a kid. The dust bunnies bred like ... well ... rabbits on the bare oak floors. Under heavy maternal orders, it seemed like I was always charging around with a dust mop seeking out and destroying dust bunny nests. Beneath my bed was a perfect hiding place for them. With my trusty dust mop I'd sweep them out …along with the occasional peach pit or apple core that told me my brother had been under my bed reading my diary AGAIN!)

My mother objected to my technique of waving the mop around over my head in a crazed victory celebration whenever I would succeed in routing all the dust bunnies out of my room.

The day I tripped over the mop and fell down a flight of stairs almost convinced my mother I was not cut out for housekeeping, but she persisted in training me for house wifely pursuits.

I mentioned all this to Susan-Up-The-Street when she talked of putting in an oak floor. Susan remembered dust bunnies too, but when I told her about my falling down the stairs after a frenzy of chasing the dusty puffs that hid under my bed, she stopped me in mid narrative to top me with her tale of jumping dust bunnies.

She was about nine and always had her nose in a book. One day she was reading a Nancy

Jane Hallock Combs

Drew mystery when out of the corner of her eye she noticed a couple of clumps of dust sort of move out from under the couch. She thought fleetingly, "Hm-m Must be a breeze," and fell back again into her Nancy Drew. Then her eye was drawn to still more dust bunnies moving across the floor. She put down her book and looked. Could there be a door open somewhere and a breeze blowing. But no. There was no breeze ... there was just this bunch of dust balls coming out from under the couch like a small fuzzy battalion ... and not just rolling out ... they were JUMPING! Jumping dust bunnies!

Suddenly Susan remembered her younger brother's collection of baby frogs he had been keeping in a box under the couch. She got down on the floor with the dust bunnies and watched them hopping onto the rug. Sure enough. That's what they were, lots of little frogs coated with layers of fuzzy dust.

When Susan's mother came into the living room she found Susan sitting cross legged on the floor with a dust cloth in her hand working on some project. Susan was always working on projects. Still is!

"What are you doing, honey?" her mother asked in all innocence.

"Dusting Jamey's frogs" was the answer. And she was. She dusted them off each and every one, then put them back in their little box.

And MY mother thought I was weird with my mop victory dance! Ha!

Cooking my Goose & Other Holiday Thoughts

Christmas is coming, the goose is getting "you know what." My family wants me to visit them in Florida for the holidays. My son-in-law, Big Christopher, even offered to drive to Kentucky, pick me up, then bring me back!

Christopher has never spent Christmas with me. I have my own traditions. I try to keep things low key. If I don't, I throw up. No joke!

When I was a kid, my parents never looked forward much to Christmas or my birthdays because I would work myself up into such a frenzy of excited anticipation that when the happy day arrived, my body would be as taut as a wire, and while everyone else was enjoying the festivities, I would be barfing my innards out. Many times I lay alone in bed, between barfing bouts, while all the world was partying. It was not really a lot of fun. My parents would try to get me to 'tone down' before Christmas and birthdays and not, 'get so worked up'.

"Remember last year," they'd say, "when you threw up all over your new Betsy Wetsy, then spent the whole day in bed sipping consommé while everyone else was downstairs having roast beef and Yorkshire Pudding (my all time favorites)?"

But "last year" was always a *long time ago* and I was certain THIS year would be better. It never was. But as time has insisted on going by in its rushing way and I've grown older, I've found that Christmases and birthdays flip by so rapidly, my times of holiday-induced intestinal distress have become fewer. I don't have *time* to work up a good frenzy.

The last time I spent a birthday tossing my cookies was when I turned forty. But I had a good excuse. I had just left Rochester and my husband of 18 years, packed my three kids and a cat into the station wagon and headed south towards

Florida and a divorce. It was difficult driving with my index finger in a cast (my former husband had slammed it in the car door shortly before I left). I still have nightmares about driving with my finger in a cast while three kids bickered about everything and jockeyed for position in the possession packed car. They shared their observations with me, like:

"Amy threw my jacket in the back and the cat's kicking kitty litter all over it!"

"Did not!"

"Did too!"

"It just FELL there!"

"It stinks in here!"

True. Through the rear view mirror, I could see the cat sitting tall again in her litter box, head held high looking like an Egyptian icon doing her best to handle the wild diarrhea which had attacked her two and a half minutes after we'd backed out of the driveway.

"How much longer till we get to Florida?" This after we'd just turned south at Binghamton, N.Y.

We made it as far as Washington before my right leg and arm collapsed and refused to respond to commands. I was also slurring words. Scared to death! I couldn't go see a doctor because I had just enough money to get me to Florida and the sanctuary of my parents condominium. I knew a doctor would slap me in the hospital and what would the kids and the cat do then? *Did I care?* Yeah, I did.

So we drove on, with my sixteen year old, armed with her temporary learner's permit, doing all the driving. Bless her.

When we got to Florida, my leg and arm were some better though my speech was not lovely. The only thing about me that was reasonably OK was my hair, which was shoulder length and slightly waved. My dear mother said, "You really need a permanent in Florida because of the heat and humidity". She would treat me to one for my upcoming birthday.

She took me into a shop which specialized in old ladies who were stylistically challenged. I came out with short, curly hair and a neck shaved practically up to the crown. I looked very old and definitely stylistically challenged.

The next day I turned forty.

I woke up in the morning, looked in the mirror and threw up. I kept doing that until about noon when we went to the emergency room and the doctor shot me full of Valium then sent me home with a jug of Valium for my mother to administer. I slept for a week solid, occasionally cracking open an eye and sipping some soup with a Valium chaser then ... back to the land of nod.

When I finally came to, I was OK... relatively speaking ... and I haven't holiday barfed in years. But I don't think I'll go to Florida for Christmas. Not this year. I'll just stay in Kentucky. I may even cook a nice, fat goose for dinner. If I can figure out a polite way to order one from the butcher.

Vermont and Lost Luggage

I'm getting ready to go to Vermont soon. I hope the airline loses my luggage! This is the third summer in a row I'll have gone to Vermont to visit old friends ... old friends who lived in France for years studying the language and ... French cooking. My French isn't very good, but there's nothing wrong with my appetite!

It's not easy to get to Vermont from Kentucky. Actually, it's almost impossible. Last year I had three stops, changed planes twice and ended the last leg in an eight person commuter plane from Boston bouncing over the mountains and lakes arriving looking more frazzled than usual. I also arrived without my luggage.

The weather in Vermont is pleasant in the summer ... not too hot, not too cold ... but one does need clothes ... I filled out the requisite lost luggage forms with Culligan Air lines (and soft water company, I believe). I was told:

"No problem! We'll have your luggage on the next plane. We'll call you. Where are you staying?"

I gave my friends', the Marx's, address and phone number then drove to Okemo Mountain hoping all would be well.

The next morning after sleeping in a borrowed nightshirt, I called the airline to see if my luggage had arrived.

"Did you fill out a lost luggage claim?"

"Of course I did." I answered

They didn't have it … the claim … or my luggage.

"We need to have the address where you'll be and the telephone number."

I gave it to them *again*.

During that first full vacation day, I called the airport several times, but each time I called, they knew me not! They also denied having any connection to my lost luggage. I called Continental. I called Boston. I thought of calling Ralph Nader ... or my mother! I was getting desperate!

Finally, I did the sensible thing. I called American Express ... to whom I had charged my flight. I like American Express. I talked to a nice, comforting lady. Actually I sobbed at her:

"I'm up here on vacation, and I'm spending all my time on the phone and no one knows anything about my luggage ... or if they do, they're not saying ... and I'm staying with friends. My friend Pat would lend me some clothes, but I'm a size twelve, and she's a four."

The lovely American Express lady said something like, "Now just stop blubbering for a minute. You're insured against luggage loss. I'll mail a lost luggage claim form to your home address ... and in the meantime you can go out and spend up to $300 for emergency clothes. Just save your receipts and mail them to us when you get home. Have a nice trip."

BLESS HER! I hung up the phone, grabbed my friend, Pat, and roared off to shop courtesy of American Express. I wanted to hurry for fear my bags would be found before I bought my "emergency clothes".

Near Pat and Rol's condo is a marvelous little Vermont village devoted to discount factory outlets ... good ones ... and since it was almost the end of their summer season ... the discount stores were having big sales! I've never had so much fun. Spending someone else's money is always nice. I bought an emergency bathing suit, a couple of gorgeous emergency dresses, slacks, shirts, etc., etc., etc. and a big, blue, blown-glass emergency ring.

Oh! With a little proding from American Express (those are good boys to have on your side!) my suitcases were finally discovered and forwarded on to me ... but my emergency clothes

Jane Hallock Combs

were mine to keep. When I got home, I filled out my claim form, sent them my receipts and received the promised $300. Nice deal.

So I'm going to Vermont again. And I hope they lose my luggage. American Express NOW pays $500 ... so I'm hoping for the worst.

The Sordid Truth About Robins!

Robins are such dreadful dissemblers. I saw one yesterday on the 7th tee at Sullivan's … looking sedate and dignified. It walked like my friend, George Lewis, taking up collection in church. Stomach thrust forward, head pulled back, walking with slow, measured steps. The soul of Episcopalian dignity.

"Ha!" I laughed watching the bird sedately stepping across the tee trying to impress the world with its "Je ne sais quoi"…

"I know you!" I muttered, "I'VE LIVED IN Florida! Don't give me that "goody-two-shoes" routine!"

Let me tell all you non-Floridians the sordid story about those innocent looking birds!

You may think you know about robins. They're pleasant, sober sorts of birds. Right? They sing. They court their beloveds in sensible, modest ways … no wild twirling and showing off like the mockingbird crew. Robins court sensibly, then procreate, raising nice, sober, pleasant, sensible families from smooth, no nonsense, blue eggs … the essence of bird purity.

Robins have a reputation for goodness which they strive to live up to with all the intensity of a dedicated Methodist. The terrible truth is that these beautiful, formal, family folks (so intent on singing songs while gleaning wormy goodies for their babies) are a totally different sort when they migrate south for the winter.

Like some humans I've met, as the robins pass Valdosta and cross into Florida, they toss all inhibitions aside. They become an entirely different species of bird from the one we all *think* we know and love.

Anywhere north of Valdosta, people look *forward* to the return of the robin with:

"Oh Goodie! I saw a ROBIN today! Spring must be coming!"

Not so in Florida. Robins are looked on as just more "snow-birds" come to sow a few wild oats before heading back north leaving a wake of wacky distruction behind.

Prepared for the truth? Here it is. In Florida, Robins are ROWDY! They are *DIRTY, MESSY DRUNKS!* That's what they are! Those sweet, sober-looking birds!

"IMPOSSIBLE!" you say.

"Possible! Probable! CERTAIN!" I say.

It shocked my northern soul to the core the first time I heard a Floridian say:

"Oh Lord, here come those robins again. Batten down the hatches, grab a broom, lock up the jewlery!"

Then I *saw* the birds!

"But that's not a robin!" I stared at the scrawny, drab colored bird teetering on the brink of my bird bath. I thought he would fall in any moment and drown. "His chest isn't even red."

"Look closely. He's got two or three reddish feathers. He's incognito. He doesn't want anyone who knows him to catch his act."

With that the bird flew on unsteady wings up to land in my holly berry bush which I noticed was alive with other drabbish looking birds. They jabbered loudly while yanking and grabbing at the ripening holly berries, snagging them off the bush and making a shambles of my pool deck. The birds also showed definite signs of INEBRIATION!

What I didn't know was that the innocuous Florida Holly Berry Bush is the bird equivalent of "Benny's Beach Bar and Grill." Those birds were stinking DRUNK!

Three of them tried to fly at once. Two crashed headlong into each other and fell to the ground … I swear LAUGHING! The third flew in an eliptical arc then bopped his head on my picture window, falling to my pool deck. He burped, then staggered off to pick up berry droppings under the now denuded berry bush.

Drunk on the fermented juice of the holly berry, they couldn't sing if they wanted. Robins in Florida almost NEVER sing! Occasionally they let out a discordant: "Blue-f-f! Blue-f-f!!," loudly, something of a bird's drunken sea chanty, but THAT's IT! The rest of the time they just stagger about burping and chirping and smearing berry seeds and naughty stuff all over pool decks. Some times they try to fly and end up doing weird loop-de-loops before landing on a branch only to fall off again!

Several actually fell into my pool. Maybe that's why they are so drab in Florida … they fall into pools and get chlorinated.

The first time I saw this performance it was funny. After 22 years, it lost its charm and I too cussed those rowdy, drunken, no good birds. At least once every tourist season, <u>The St. Petersburg</u>

<u>Times</u> does an article about those "drunken" robins. It's a grim and nasty story ... but it is true.

Yesterday, as I looked at the bird on Sullivan's 7th tee, I thought again about how similar birds and humans are. You would never think that bird capable of roudyism, but look again! Under that sedate exterior lies a craving for holly berries and hooliganism! ... And that beautiful red breast is probably just holly berry stains left over from last winter!

Echoes of Spring

It's a spring morning. A quiet spring morning. Early. I let the dog out … the LARGE, yellow dog. The tremendous, yellow dog with the huge voice.

Sam, said dog, has done his warm-up stretching in the house. He likes to get the fundamentals out of the way. Then, when I open the door, he launches himself into the world with all the power of a space shuttle blasting off, and in a moment the peace of the quiet morning is shattered into little, shiny shards.

Sam barks at birds, at squirrels, at anything that has the temerity to move in the morning, but mostly he barks at the big vicious dog who lives on the hill across the way. The big, vicious dog barks back.

"Woof, woof, woof!" from Sam.

"Woof, woof, woof!" from other dog.

Sam escalates things. Tags on another woof or two. Big vicious dog does the same. Sam races across our lawn, hurling invective and his big voice at the dog he cannot see.

Of course he can't. We live on a hill. Sam's barking at his echo on the other hill. He's been doing it for years. I keep trying to tell him that it's just his big voice that is answering him. He doesn't believe me, or else he can't hear my words because he is too busy keeping that big dog at bay.

I am safe from that big dog ... and echoes. At least I'm safe from Sam's echoes. Of my own echoes I'm not so sure.

A writer is a lot like a dog on a hill in the morning ... throwing words into the air to disappear into nothingness or richochet back at you. Words can hurt! It makes me want to give up at times … and maybe I will … but I'll wait until the postman comes. Hope always springs upon me. Maybe there'll be something in the mail!

I walk with Sam as the day wakens. Birds and animals are stirring. Sure. Sam woke them. We walk down the dirt road that runs between the hills. Sam runs five miles while I walk one. Back and forth he tears through field and stream. A dog's delight. A run in the morning.

It's a gorgeous day. Not a cloud in view. The air's still crisp. It'll be warm soon, but for now the cool breeze stirs the trees and Sam … and me. We wander up the echo hill. No dog here.

"See, Sam?"

Sam doesn't see. He's too busy. He's after a squirrel. That squirrel better watch out.

Time to get home and get back to work. We make it up our hill again to our own house.

It's been a lovely spring. It's been a horrible spring. My husband, Bill, died in March. Sam misses him. So do I. I throw his name out into the bright morning. But all that comes back is an echo.

~~~~~~

In Memorium - Bill Combs 1933-1997

About The Author

A graduate of St. Lawrence University, Canton, N.Y., Ms. Combs has written short stories and articles for many newspapers and magazines.

Her books include *Please Pass the Watermelon, I've got a Headache, My Brother Dave, Cooking Runs in the Family, but not far Enough, and No Kidding, a Primer for Teachers/tutors New to Adult Education* published by Longmuir/Jones Publishing, *Mysteries*, published by Harcourt, Brace, Jovanovich; and the five book ESOL series *English: Your Second Language* published by Steck-Vaughn Publishing. She lives and writes in West Kentucky.